GUIDE TO BETTER GARDENING

GALAHAD BOOKS

FRESH FRUITS AND VEGETABLES

Editor: Margaret Verner
Dust Jacket designed by Roswita Busskamp
Copyright © 1981 by 'Round the World Books Inc.

Fresh Fruits and Vegetables published by
Galahad Books Inc., New York City.

This edition published by arrangement with
'Round the World Books Inc., New York, N.Y.

Library of Congress Catalog Card Number: 79-56676
ISBN: 0-88365-437-7
Printed in the United States of America

PICTURE ACKNOWLEDGEMENTS

A.B. Morse: 12T, 23, 25, 26, 40, 41R, 42B, 43T, 44, 53T, 55 —Horticultural Experiment Station, Vineland, Ont.: 10T,
18TL, 18TR, 18BL, 18BR, 27T, 32BL, 33T, 38B — Joseph Harris Co. Inc., Rochester, N.Y.: 6, 7, 9T, 15T, 29, 31, 34B,
36, 38T, 59R, 63TL, 69T, 69B, 70, 71B, 72, 75T, 75B, 77T, 78, 79L, 80T, 80BR, 83T, 83B, 84C, 84R, 86B, 87, 89T,
89BR, 89BL, 90T, 90B, 91B, 92TL, 92B, 93TL, 93B, 94TL, 94B — Keith Seeds, Toronto, Ont.: 58, 61T — Kelly Bros.,
Dansville, N.Y.: 45, 49B, 51L, 56L — New York State Experimental Station, Geneva, N.Y.: 9B, 10B, 11B, 12B, 13T, 13B,
15B, 16T, 16B, 17TR, 17B, 19T, 19B, 20, 21, 22T, 22B, 27B, 28, 30T, 30B, 32T, 32BR, 33BL, 33BR — Ontario
Agricultural College, Guelph, Ont.: 35, 62B, 65, 66, 67, 74B, 80BL, 88T, 95T, 95B — Stark Bros., Louisiana, Mo.: 11T,
17TL, 41L, 42T, 43B, 46T, 46B, 47, 48T, 48B, 49T, 50T, 50B, 51R, 52T, 52B, 53B, 54T, 54B, 56R — Stokes Seed Co., St.
Catherines, Ont.: 73 — W. Atlee Burpee Co., Philadelphia, Pa.: 34T, 37, 57, 59L, 60R, 63B, 64, 68, 71T, 74T, 76, 77B,
79R, 81, 82, 84L, 85, 86T, 88B, 91T, 92TR, 93TR, 94TR, 96.

Table of Contents

FRUITS 5

ALL ABOUT GROWING BERRIES 6

RASPBERRIES 7
Care of Raspberries 8
Red Raspberries 9
Everbearing Raspberries 9
Black and Purple Raspberries 11

BLUEBERRIES 12

ALL ABOUT STRAWBERRIES 12
June-bearing Strawberries 18
Everbearing Strawberries 20

BLACKBERRIES 22

GOOSEBERRIES 23

THORNLESS BOYSENBERRY 24

BLACK & RED CURRANTS 25

ALL ABOUT GRAPES 27
Care of grape vines 28
White Grapes 29
Red Grapes 30
Black Grapes 31

MUSKMELONS OR CANTALOUPES 34
Warm Climate Melons 36

WATERMELONS 36

RHUBARB 38

FRUIT TREES 39

Apple Trees 41
Pear Trees 44
Plum and Prune Trees 46
Cherry Trees 49
Peach Trees 51
Apricot Trees 54
Dwarf fruit trees 55

VEGETABLES 57

Planning the garden 58
Planting & care of vegetables 61
Transplanted vegetables 64
Cultivation 66
Mulching 67
Watering 67
Feeding 67
A late vegetable garden 68

THE HOME VEGETABLE GARDEN **68**
Garden Peas 68
Tomatoes 71
Snap beans 77
Lima Beans 79
Beets 80
Asparagus 81
Cucumbers 82
Radishes 84
Lettuce 85
Onions 87
Carrots 87
Corn 90
Cabbage 92
Squash 93
Potatoes 95
Swiss Chard 96

FRUITS

FRUITS

The strawberry is the most popular fruit grown in the Western hemisphere.

ALL ABOUT GROWING BERRIES

Most pleasant memories are of little things. Nearly everyone has the mouth-watering recollection of eating fresh pluck-ed strawberries or raspberries, of biting into a crisp apple right off the tree. Such recollections leave a yearning with most gardeners to ultimately own a fabulous orchard or luscious berry-patch of their own. However, in most cities and towns the

gardens are usually too small for such dreams and so the would-be fruit fancier has to confine his activities to growing small fruits.

The various small fruits such as straw-berries, raspberries, black currants, etc., can be successfully grown by anyone, even by beginners to gardening. With the modern development of fast freezing, the berries

would not only be enjoyed while in season, but will add a delightful taste treat any other time of the year.

Buy the best stock — When making your purchases of small fruit stock, buy the best — normally there is very little differ-ence in price between good stock and poor. Find out from your local Garden Club or Horticultural Society the best varieties to grow and the better suppliers in your area.

Resist the temptation of taking some of your neighbour's old stock. In many cases the plants and bushes are eithei old or are diseased.

Berries require good soil — The one big factor in growing any berry crop suc-cessfully is properly prepared soil. There are no small fruits which will flourish in very poor soils containing little humus.

Sandy or heavy clay requires the addi-tion of humus and the best form of humus for small fruits is well rotted barnyard manure. Admittedly this is not readily available in large cities, but it is worth the trouble of seeking it out. If you live near a place where mushrooms are commercially grown, the manure discarded after a crop of mushrooms has been produced is good for enriching the soil before planting small fruits. The next best form of humus to use would be one of the materials processed from sewage. Peat moss and material from the home compost heap are also suitable.

In very poor soils the humus can be safely applied at the rate of 8 to 10 bushels per hundred square feet of bed area. At the same time, work into the soil a complete fertilizer at the rate of 4 pounds per hun-dred square feet.

Berry plants or bushes require little or no spraying or dusting. Provided you buy disease free stock from a reliable nursery in the beginning, you should not have any trouble from disease or insect pests.

RASPBERRIES

Raspberries are worthy of a place in any garden; they are easy to grow and care for, present no problem to the beginner and the berries, usually borne in profusion are delicious either fresh, frozen or preserved. There are four kinds, red, white, purple and black, of these red is the most popular, and easiest on the gardener. They are also the most hardy, although in this respect you must remember that all raspberries are susceptible to heat and drought.

Planting—Raspberries require a moist, well-drained soil which has been well supplied with humus. If you set them out in soil containing plenty of humus and plant food, your raspberries will go on producing fruit for ten to twelve years without replanting. Compare this with strawberries which must be re-planted every year for successful fruiting.

Choose a location in your garden which will be more or less permanent and where the bushes will receive full sunshine.

The preparation of the soil for planting is a very simple job. Dig into the soil a minimum of 6 to 8 bushels of humus as outlined earlier in the book. At the same time, also work into the soil a complete fertilizer at the rate of 4 pounds per hundred square feet. Mix the humus, fertilizer and soil thoroughly together.

For a small bed, this can be easily done with a spade, but for a large area, it will probably be more advisable to either rent a small rotary tiller, or hire a man who does custom rotary tilling. The results of rotary tilling are particularly good, because the humus, soil and fertilizer will be thoroughly mixed down to a depth of 8 inches. Furthermore, the soil is left in a ready-to-plant condition.

Before planting you will have to rake the soil, because rotary tilling leaves the soil in a puffed up condition.

Spring or Fall? — Planting time for raspberries is either very early in the Spring, or in the Fall. However, except in the extremely cold areas, where sub-zero temperatures are regularly experienced, the best time for planting raspberries is in the Fall. This is the time the commercial grower does his planting, and we can always learn from him.

There are four kinds of raspberries—red, black, purple and white.

In the case of Spring planting, you will have to get the raspberry canes in the soil just as soon as the soil is workable. The reason for this extra early planting is to take advantage of the speed at which the raspberry canes grow when the weather turns warm. This means you should place your order with the nursery in January, February or early March to be sure of having the stock delivered in time.

The distance to plant apart is 3 feet in the row and 6 feet between rows. When making the planting hole, dig it 3 inches deeper than needed and place a small handful of complete fertilizer in the bottom. Cover this with 2 inches of soil to prevent the roots coming in direct contact with the fertilizer. If this should happen, some burning of the roots would undoubtedly take place, and the plants would be either seriously injured or killed.

Set the plants at the same depth as they were in the nursery. This can be accomplished by observing the soil line appearing just above the roots on the bark of the cane. When planting, make sure you take good care to firm the soil well around the roots.

This is done to eliminate any air pockets which would prevent the roots from taking hold quickly and starting to grow. But at the same time, you must be careful not to injure the roots and the newly growing shoots.

Severe pruning is essential—The next step is to cut off the canes one foot above the ground immediately after planting. The beginner may not relish this phase of planting but it is necessary and beneficial to the cane.

By pruning down to one foot, the lower buds will be forced to throw out growth, thus producing stockier plants which will produce larger and more fruit. When blossom time comes along, remove all the blooms so that no fruits will form the first year. Again, this is a particularly hard task for many people to perform. It is much better to sacrifice the fruit the first year to enable the canes to become well established. The energy which would go into producing fruits is much better chanelled into producing good root systems and huskier plants which in turn will bear a bigger crop of berries the second year.

Care of plants — Earlier we said that raspberries grow very quickly in the Spring, this is the time to feed the canes. Feed with a complete fertilizer at the rate of one pound per 25 square feet of row area. Spread the fertilizer on either side of the row and gently work it into the soil. Since raspberries are very shallow rooted, the best tool for the job is a garden rake.

When the leaves begin to break out on the already established canes, cut them back, leaving two-thirds of their length.

The reason for waiting until the leaves appear is to find out whether any Winter killing has taken place. The canes are cut back one-third to prevent them growing too long and flopping over, under the weight of the fruit.

Weeding is important — About the middle of June give the bushes a final thorough cultivation to remove any weeds. Follow up by laying down a mulch of clean wheat straw covering all the ground where the bushes are planted. To be effective, this mulch should be two to three inches deep. The mulch will serve to keep the area free of weeds, and materially help to preserve moisture in the soil during the fruiting season when the weather is hot and dry. It also makes a clean surface on which to set berry boxes or other containers and for kneeling on while picking or otherwise caring for the raspberries.

Later on in the Fall the straw can be dug into the top four or five inches of soil and so add considerable humus. The following Spring it will be necessary to apply a fertilizer high in nitrogen. The soil will have used up its nitrogen in breaking down the wheat straw into humus.

Remove all old canes — After the final berries are picked, the canes that produced the berries should be cut down to the ground level.

Older canes can become carriers of diseases and insect pests if left in position for any length of time, particularly if left over until the following Spring.

Canes which have been cut out should be burned, and not consigned to the home compost heap. It is true they are sufficiently fibrous to break down into humus if cut in small pieces and placed in the home compost box, but because of their disease and insect-carrying possibilities, they are much better burned when removed from the bushes. Old canes are extremely inflammable and burn with tremendous heat, it is therefore wiser to keep the fire some distance away from shrubs, trees, plants or buildings.

Perhaps the easiest and safest way is to cut them in small pieces and place them in the incinerator.

Care of Raspberries

Set out plants in Spring or Fall, keeping them 3′ apart in rows 5 to 6 feet apart.

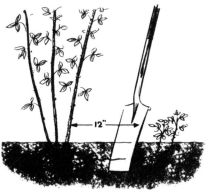

Propagate by sucker growth from roots. Prune roots by the use of a spade.

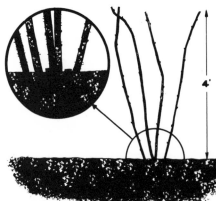

Prune tops of the plants after growth begins in the Spring. Cut back to 3 or 4 feet and allow 4 canes to a plant.

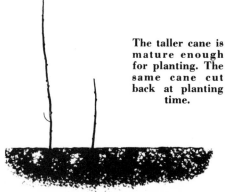

The taller cane is mature enough for planting. The same cane cut back at planting time.

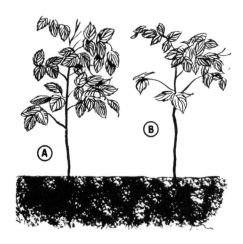

Plant "A" is a good sucker type for planting. Plant "B" is a poor type, showing sparse root and no underground stem.

8

Red Raspberries

Latham — More Latham raspberry canes have been planted and are still being planted than any other variety. No other red raspberry is so popular or profitable. Having originated in Minnesota, the bushes are extremely hardy and long-lasting.

45° below zero temperatures have had no harmful effects on this extra fine variety. Latham is free from insects and diseases, and multiplies rapidly. The fact that it is free from the virus disease "mosaic" is an important point in its favor. Berries are exceptionally large, plump, juicy — have a delicious flavor, and are free from seediness. Bushes are loaded to the ground with great crops borne on clusters the entire length of the canes.

You will get a good crop of fruit the second year after planting. The berries start to ripen between July 1st and July 10th.

Viking — A vigorous grower and a very good cropper. The berries are large and firm and extremely good when eaten fresh. However, the color of the Viking berries is not as red as might be in preserves. Most of the original testing work on the fast freezing of fruits was carried out with Viking and it is still the best raspberry for that purpose. Berries are ready for picking around the 1st to the 4th of July.

Golden Amber — This new raspberry has already established a reputation as being the sweetest of all raspberries.

Bushes produce large berries which are a beautiful amber yellow in color. The berries are as large as any other raspberry, do not crumble and are of good quality. The unusual amber color has a definite appeal when offered for sale in fruit markets and roadside stands. Berries start to ripen about the middle of July, thus extending the home-grown raspberry season.

Milton is a late variety, very useful for both home and market use. Berries ripen about the 10th of July, are large, attractive bright red in color and firm without any tendency to crumble. Plants are vigorous, productive, hardy and have remained free from mosaic.

Taylor — One of the best of the red raspberries. The berries are a bright eye-

Sweet September will provide at least two crops a year

catching red, thick fleshed, firm of excellent quality and held well above the ground by sturdy canes. Housewives will praise Taylor, because it stays whole after canning and has a very enjoyable flavor. Plants are vigorous, hardy, productive, tall-growing increase rapidly. You will be able to start picking the berries some time during the first week in July.

sweet and choice, the quality being much better in the Fall than in the Summer.

Sweet September was developed and introduced by Professor George L. Slate of the New York State Experiment Station. This Station has long been known for leadership in developing new and successful bearing fruits. Plants are healthy, vigorous and hardy.

Everbearing Raspberries

Everbearing raspberries require no special care other than that for ordinary varieties.

Sweet September is the newest and best everbearing red raspberry. It will produce an abundant crop in June followed by a crop of equal size in September. Fruits ripen earlier and are as large as any of the standard varieties. The berries are very

Black raspberries—ideal for freezing

9

Indian Summer — A very fine ever-bearing red raspberry which also gives two crops in the one season; a big crop in June and another, even bigger, in September and October. Plants are medium upright, very vigorous and unusually hardy.

Some commercial growers cut their plants back to the ground early in the Spring. They are willing to sacrifice the June crop in order to get an extremely bountiful crop of giant sized berries in the Fall. This of course, is at a time when red raspberries are very scarce and these big, deliciously flavored juicy berries command high prices.

Durham — An everbearing red raspberry bearing the usual crop of fruit in early Summer, followed by another in September which continues until frost.

The berries are not as large as the Sweet September variety but have a bright red color and good quality. Durham is the hardiest and the heaviest producer of all the red everbearers. They are delicious for eating fresh, for making pies or jam and for freezing.

Purple Autumn—This is the first ever-bearing purple raspberry. The Illinois Agricultural Experiment Station created this purple raspberry having fruits which can be picked all season long from early Summer until the snow flies. A few plants will produce all the berries you require for luscious pies, shortcakes, jams and jellies.

Purple Autumn starts to bear exceptionally large individual berries, which are high in flavor and free from crumbling, in early Summer, on vigorous stocky plants with large, smooth attractive leaves. This new variety is free from disease, hardy and produces quantities of exhibition fruits.

Among their latest developments, our plant breeders have introduced everbearing varieties of raspberries which produce two crops each year. They fruit at the same time as the standard varieties, the berries being produced on the old canes. Then in September the new canes start bearing and continue until stopped by hard frost.

Viking is one of the best varieties for freezing

After fruiting, the two year old canes die and should be removed

10

Starking Black Giant will produce a crop even during hot, dry seasons

Black & Purple Raspberries

The black raspberry or black cap is a native of North America. It is found on the borders of woods from the Province of Ontario to the Carolinas, but it is not known when it was first brought into cultivation.

Purple raspberries are hybrids between black and red raspberries.

Black and purple raspberries are more demanding with regard to soil conditions. They do best in a loam or sandy loam soil which must be well drained and containing plenty of humus and fertilizer.

These varieties rarely form suckers as do all red raspberries, instead the tips of the canes bend over to the ground and when firmed into the soil, allow the formation of roots. It is these rooted tips that are used for propagation.

The time to start is in August when the canes have grown long enough to permit the operation. The best way to go about this, is to take a shovel and work up the soil, dig a hole and place two or three inches of the stem tip into it. Be sure that the soil is firmed well around the tip so there are no air holes. In the Spring cut the new plants free from the mother plant while their buds are still dormant, leaving 7 or 8 inches of the old cane as a handle to facilitate replanting in another part of the garden.

The cane should be cut away at the ground level after planting.

Require different pruning — The method of pruning black and purple raspberries also is different from red raspberries. The berries are produced on the new wood which develops as side branches or laterals on the previous year's canes. The young canes have to be cut back to 18 to 24 inches to encourage the formation of sturdy side branches.

Pruning stimulates the development of strong, leafy lateral shoots which bear flower clusters at their end.

After fruiting, the two year old canes die and should be removed as in the case of red raspberries.

Bristol — Bristol has the reputation of being the best mid-season black raspberry. Berries are large, firm, fairly glossy and of excellent quality. They have a delicious flavor with a rich tartness which makes them a favorite for eating fresh, desserts, pies, canning and freezing. Bristol starts to ripen in early June and continues for about a month.

If planted early in the Spring, it will start to bear within 15 months. The large, vigorous upright plants do not need staking. Fine for both home garden and commercial use.

Dundee — Is a promising new black raspberry notable for its high quality. Berries are big, glossy black, moderately firm and the flavor is mildly sub-acid. The tall plants are vigorous, productive and have fair resistance against the virus disease mosaic.

Cumberland — Cumberland has been the standard black raspberry for the longest period, and is the best known of all blacks.

Plants are extraordinarily productive, extremely hardy and vigorous. Fruit is extra large, of the highest quality, and firm. Cumberland is wonderful for eating fresh and for use in pies, canning or freezing.

Starking Black Giant (Stauffer) — This extremely hardy variety is a new black raspberry which will produce a crop even during very hot and dry seasons. One young plant has produced six quarts of the giant sized berries. Color is purplish black, resembling Bristol, but the berries are better and are borne more freely. The berries keep their large size throughout the season and maintain their flavor, which is rich and sub-acid. Wonderful for eating, desserts, canning, freezing and marketing.

Milton is a late variety

BLUEBERRIES

The current trend to move out to the country from the city is very often prompted by the desire to have a first class garden in which could be grown delicious fruits and vegetables. Amongst those who have achieved their ambition, and with those who are content with a small berry patch in the corner of their city garden, the growing of blueberries is becoming popular.

Being a wild rocky country berry, home garden grown blueberries have been almost impossible until very recently. With new methods and varieties which have been developed recently it is now possible for the average person living in town or country to grow their own luscious and juicy large-sized blueberries.

Blueberries have a special soil requirement — the soil has to be acid and since most home gardeners have sweetened their soil with lime to make other plants flourish, their efforts with blueberries could be unknowingly doomed to failure.

It is not hard to change the soil to contain the amount of acidity needed. A good method is to dig a hole approximately two feet square and two feet deep for each plant. Replace the soil removed with a mixture consisting of equal parts of good topsoil, sand and peat moss, which should be well mixed and moistened. Immediately before planting, add aluminum sulphate to the top of the soil using three tablespoonsful per plant, making sure it is well watered in. Apply three more feedings of the aluminum sulphate during the growing season, using the same amount each time.

Besides producing delectable fruits for desserts, the blueberry can also be a very pretty ornamental bush. It can be planted in hedge rows, or as an individual shrub in the mixed border or foundation planting.

Pollination must be taken into account, in order for the bushes to bear fruit. It takes 3 or more plants set close together, to ensure perfect fertilization of the blossoms.

A fine bush of home-grown blueberries

ALL ABOUT STRAWBERRIES

There is very little doubt that the strawberry is the most popular fruit grown in the Western hemisphere. Indeed, strawberries have been a favorite garden delicacy for at least 400 years, but it was not until the discovery of a large-fruited kind about the year 1785 that any real progress was made in developing large size varieties.

Strawberries require care

There are two kinds of strawberries suitable for growing in the home garden; those bearing a single crop each year and usually listed in the nursery catalogs as "June bearing" and the ever-bearing varieties which produce a big crop at the usual time in June and then fruit lightly all through Summer and Autumn.

Preparation of the soil — Strawberries prefer a sandy, loamy soil rich in humus and fertilizer but good results can be obtained in almost any type of soil which has been properly prepared. As soon as the soil is workable in the Spring, apply a complete fertilizer at the rate of 4 pounds per hundred square feet. On top of this scatter one of the forms of humus at the rate of 6 to 8 bushels per hundred square feet. The rate of application can be increased to 10 to 12 bushels per hundred square feet if the soil is not very good. For strawberries, well-rotted barnyard manure or discarded mushroom manure are by far

Everbearing strawberries are usually grown on the hill system

leaving a plant having two or three bright green leaves.

The matted row system of planting is the most suited for home gardens. The rows are spaced three feet apart and the plants one and a half to two feet, depending on the variety. Ask the nurseryman from whom you buy your plants, the correct planting distance for the variety you have selected. Under the matted row system, runners thrown out by the mother plants are permitted to set new plants 4 to 6 inches from each other until the matted row is 18 inches to two feet wide. All other runners should be destroyed.

Larger fruit will result if care is taken to keep only the early formed runner plants, and the rows are limited to a width of 12 to 15 inches.

The "hill system" in which all runners are removed as they form and before they root is another common way of growing strawberries. Every two or three days, you will have to go through your strawberry plants and remove the runners with a sharp knife or pruner. Plants grown under this method, have more room, are very vigorous, and develop very strong crowns. Berries are consistently larger and very good crops are obtained. This is the way to grow the ever-

the best forms of humus to use, but unfortunately, in many large cities and towns, these are not readily available. Materials processed from sewage, peat moss or compost are good substitutes if manures are not available. The fertilizer can be either spaded or rotary tilled into the soil. The best results are obtained from rotary tilling because these machines thoroughly mix together the soil, the humus and the fertilizer, and the bed is left in a ready-to-plant condition. After rotary tilling the soil should receive a final raking before planting takes place.

Fall planted strawberries give better yields—Strawberries can be planted in the Spring during the last two weeks in April or the first week in May, but the proven best time of planting them is the Fall.

Fall planted strawberries send out runners earlier in the Spring and in greater numbers than Spring-set plants. It is these early runners that produce most of the fruit the following season.

October is the month to plant the berries, when other garden and farm work is less pressing and the soil usually in better condition than in the Spring. About the only disadvantages of Fall planting is the extra

mulching the plants require to prevent Winter damage. However, this is not too big a

Empire should be grown only for fresh use

problem in the home garden where the number of plants is small.

Buy your plants from a recognized nursery of good standing, or from a commercial fruit grower who specializes in raising clean, healthy plants. Be sure to specify that you wish virus-free plants.

Planting — When the plants come from the nursery, they are usually covered with old, brownish leaves and may have the previous year's runners still clinging to them. Strip off all old growth before planting,

bearing varieties.

Planting strawberries requires two people working together. One pushes a spade six or seven inches into the ground at the right location and moves it back and forth to make a planting hole. The soil is drawn back while the other person inserts the roots in the cavity created so that they fan out against the wall of the hole. The spade is then withdrawn and the soil is pushed forward against the roots, and firmed down with the heel.

A first class strawberry plant trimmed for planting, showing plenty of young white roots.

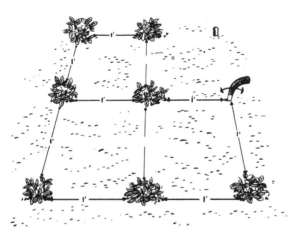

For the hill system set plants on corners of 1' x 1' squares and for larger plantings skip every 4th or 5th row for a 2' picking alley.

STRAW MULCH

Mulch plants with straw 2" to 3" deep for cleaner healthier fruit.

TOO LOW   TOO HIGH   RIGHT

Make a hole 6" deep—set plants with roots straight down. See that the crown is level with top of soil.

Planting depth is very important for strawberries, extreme care must be taken to ensure that the middle of the crown is even with the surface of the soil.

The crown must not be covered or the roots exposed — It is also important to make sure the roots of the plants are kept moist during the planting operation. If the tender rootlets are exposed to the sun or wind for more than a minute or so, they will be seriously injured. Keep the roots moist by covering them with a wet piece of burlap or by carrying them in a pail of water.

Most June-bearing strawberry plants will produce blossoms the first year after planting, and if these were left on the plants they would produce some berries. However, this is another one of those occasions in the garden when one must be ruthless and remove the blossoms as they appear. The plants will require all their energy to become established and form a fruiting crown for a crop the next year. If some of this energy is expended by producing fruit the first year, the next season's crop will be much smaller.

Feeding new plants — Three or four weeks after planting is the time to give the

Sparkle has a quality reputation

Be sure of correct planting distance for the variety you select

plants their first feeding with a complete fertilizer at the rate of three pounds per hundred square feet of row. Make sure any grains of fertilizer which may be on the leaves is brushed off with a broom or whisk to prevent the leaves from being burned. Work the fertilizer into the soil with a hoe then give the plants a good soaking to dissolve the plant food and see that it is carried down to the roots of the plants. During the middle of August another feeding is required to stimulate the formation of fruit buds. If possible use a fertilizer high in nitrogen, such as nitrate of soda or sulphate of ammonia. Nitrate of soda is the best for this purpose because it can be broadcast over and around the plants on any dry day. You will discover that on such a day very little of the fertilizer will stick to the foliage and what does remain can be

15

easily brushed off. The nitrate of soda must be cultivated into the soil followed by giving the plants a good soaking. They will have received a good soaking when the water has penetrated to a depth of five or six inches.

Strawberries require plenty of care — Strawberries need to be cultivated frequently to keep weeds under control and to make sure that the surface of the soil is kept fine and crumbly so that the developing runners will be able to root easily in its surface. Strawberries are easier to cultivate than most plants because you can use the hoe right up to the plant as the roots grow straight down into the ground. While hoeing or doing any of the other necessary jobs in your strawberry bed, take time to direct and place the runners where you want them.

It is impossible for strawberries to produce a big crop of large berries if the soil starts to dry out. You can have plenty of rainfall until a week or so before picking is to start, and then if a hot, dry spell comes along, your chances of getting a successful crop would be very slim. If rainfall is not adequate, strawberries require a good soaking once a week from the time they are set out in the Spring until some time in October. Best way of watering strawberries is to use one of the new canvas or plastic soakers. Holes in the material allow the water to ooze out slowly at a rate the earth can absorb. The porous canvas soakers are probably better to use because no spray of water is created to wet leaves and fruit. This materially helps to lessen the spread of leaf and fruit diseases.

Mulching — Strawberry plants can be injured by extremely cold Winter temperatures, or by heaving caused by intermittent thawing and freezing in late Winter and early Spring. No trouble on this account is experienced if a correct mulch is applied. The mulch will also shelter the crowns and the roots from the drying action of Winter winds. Clean wheat, rye or oat straw makes the best mulch for strawberries, because it does not pack tightly over the plants and smother them. When we say "clean" wheat straw we refer to the possibility of bringing extra weeds to the garden in one of these mulch materials. A big crop of weeds will use up valuable moisture and plant food consequently the quality and the crop of

A mulch of clean wheat straw prevents berries being covered with soil

strawberries will be materially reduced. Apply the mulch after the plants have become dormant. This will be after the first severe frost, but before the temperature falls to around 20°. Naturally the time to apply such a mulch will vary with the climate in your area, but in most places it will be some time in November. Spread the material 2 to 3 inches deep. Don't apply too much straw or you may smother the plants.

The mulch must be allowed to remain on the plants until the frosty weather of early Spring is over. In any case it should not be removed as long as the plants remain dormant. Remove when new leaf growth appears and the foliage begins to become yellowish in color. The mulch is pulled back from the plants and left in the pathways between the rows. This serves to help keep the berries clean, conserve moisture, and to provide a clean place on which to set boxes or containers, or to kneel.

In European countries straw has been used for generations as a mulch and its use gave strawberries their name.

If you are fortunate enough to have a saw-mill or a lumber yard nearby, you should be able to obtain a supply of sawdust which makes a very fine mulch for strawberries. It should be applied in November after the first severe frost and before the temperature falls below 20°. Spread the mulch to a depth of 2 to 3 inches.

In breaking down into humus, sawdust requires large amounts of nitrogen to feed the decomposition bacteria. This means the surrounding soil will be robbed of nitrogen

Strawberries grown in the row system

16

Starkrimson has a luscious flavor

Pocahontas—excellent for freezing

to the detriment of the plants and crop of fruit. To counteract this, apply additional nitrate of soda in the early Spring. Any nitrogen thus applied would be in addition to any other nitrogen fertilizing required for producing the strawberry crop.

Renewing the strawberry bed — It is good gardening **practice** to relocate your strawberry bed every year. This is best done after the season is over. The quality and the size of the fruits obtained will be very much better as the plants are not so thick in the row and the bed can be kept free of weeds. In many areas these days the white grub is troublesome and it is most important to set out a new bed every year as this pest increases rapidly in old plantations.

In order to set out a new bed every year there will be an approximate two month period when you have two strawberry beds on the go — one bearing fruit in June and a new planting which will not bear until the following June. When you dig up the old bed as soon as it has finished bearing, it can be replaced with a Fall crop of beans, carrots, radishes or beets.

Empire—mid-season to late variety

Renovating an old bed—It is possible to get two crops of fruit from the one bed and this is recommended for gardens where space is limited and the strawberry bed is kept free of weeds. When the bearing season is over, rake up the straw between the rows and move it off to one side, then ruthlessly cut down each row to a width of about 15 inches. Gather up and destroy the plants, then go through the bed and meticulously remove any weeds present. Follow up with a feeding of nitrate of soda which can be broadcast over the plants, brushed off the leaves and watered into the ground with a good soaking. Cultivate the bed frequently throughout the remainder of the year, and by Fall the bed should be in good condition once more. The plants will need the same kind of mulch as they received the first year, some time during the month of November.

Protection from the birds — There is nothing more frustrating for the home gardener than to go to all the trouble and expense of developing a good strawberry bed and then have the birds steal most of the berries. Many remedies have been tried. Strawberry growers often use carbide "guns" which make a loud bank at regular intervals, but this is not feasible in cities, towns or villages where the noise would annoy nearby neighbours.

For the home garden, the best protection would be a covering of chicken wire, used fish net, or other material which would not exclude too much light and sunshine.

June~bearing Strawberries

Earlidawn — It is the first of all high quality June-bearing strawberries to ripen. Berries are large size and an appetizing bright red in color. The flesh is firm, sweet and delicious. A recent introduction of the United States Department of Agriculture, it is a nearly frostproof variety. Yield tests have been well above the average, and good size is maintained throughout the fruiting season. Plants are hardy and vigorous.

Sparkle — A mid-season variety originating at the New Jersey Experiment Station. The quality of Sparkle is the very highest and is an excellent variety for freezing. The plants are vigorous and produce runners freely. You will get an excellent crop every year. Berries are of good size and an attractive, bright glossy red in color. Sparkle has an extra long fruiting season.

Earlidawn is first of the high quality June-bearing strawberries to ripen

Glossy red Sparkle berries

Premier, a popular favorite

New Midland is a fine early variety

18

New Midland — A new very high flavored berry which is achieving a wide reputation for quality. It also has outstanding size, beauty, productivity, firmness and freezing ability. Berries are large, deep glossy red, full of rich strawberry sweetness. Freezing tests show New Midland to be one of the very best for home or commercial use, remaining firm textured and will not mush when thawed.

Pocahontas is one of the best developments of the United States Department of Agriculture and ripens in early mid-season. Has large, deep vivid red berries which are extremely sweet flavored. Pocahontas is excellent for freezing.

Catskill — This variety received an Award of Merit from the Massachusetts Horticultural Society when it was first introduced. Berries are ripe in mid-season. Fruit is large to very-large in size. Color is an attractive dark, glossy red. Many persons like the taste because it is low in acidity and sweet. The plants of Catskill are large, vigorous and the yield is very abundant.

A new strawberry bed should be set out each Spring

New Midland has outstanding quality and firmness

Empire — This is a fine new strawberry created by the New York Experiment Station. Ripening time is mid-season to late. It produces huge berries over an unusually long season. In small gardens where the space is limited, Empire will give the most fruit in the least space. It should be grown for fresh use only. Berries are of excellent quality and extra big in size. The fruits are firm, hold their appearance well and will stand adverse growing conditions.

New Midway—Here we have one of the best all-purpose strawberries. Plants are exceptionally productive. It would be hard to find plants so big and vigorous, or berries so bright shiny red, clear through to the core. The big, luscious berries are honeysweet all the way through, and retain their firmness and fine appearance long after picking.

Premier — Premier has been a popular favorite ever since it was introduced in 1909 and is still the leading commercial berry in the eastern part of North America.

Everbearing Strawberries

1. Spade inserted and 6″ hole opened

2. Placing plant in position

3. Pressing soil against roots

Everbearing strawberries bear fruit from June until frost

Strawberries are available in quantity during June and early July in most parts of eastern North America. From then on, they are usually obtainable only in the fresh frozen, canned forms or as expensive fresh fruits from California.

All this has been changed with the recent introduction of some excellent ever-bearing varieties which make it possible to pick deliciously flavored strawberries from June until the hard frosts of late Fall.

Everbearing strawberries are not only useful in providing tasty desserts, but also have definite landscape possibilities as the plants make a most useful and attractive ground cover. The glossy green leaves, pretty white flowers and bright red fruits make a delightful picture.

Planted in the hill system, everbearing strawberries make excellent edgings for a walk. They will not be out of place if set in clumps along the front of the mixed border, or placed in window or planting boxes.

Many city gardens have limited space, and here the "pyramid" garden would be excellent. This consists of five aluminum rings with the largest one at the bottom being six feet in diameter, and the smallest one at the top being 4 feet, 2 inches. The planting space between the individual rings is 5 inches wide. The largest one is placed on the ground and filled with a specially prepared soil mixture. This would consist of two parts good topsoil and one part humus. To each bushel of soil add a large handful of a complete fertilizer. Then place

4. Firming soil around plant

It pays to buy only virus free plants

the next ring inside the first, fill with soil and repeat the process until all rings are in place. The resulting five bands of planting space will hold from 50 to 75 everbearing plants. This type of pyramidal garden can be planted not only with everbearing strawberries, but in combination with annuals, and vegetables. For areas where birds prove a nuisance to would-be strawberry growers, the new pyramidal gardens have support strips which will hold sufficient netting to cover the entire planting. This will not only provide positive protection from the birds, but in the Wintertime will keep straw, hay or other types of mulch in place when used as Winter protection.

Plastic pyramid covers are also available and can be used as a cold frame or greenhouse for early planting and frost protection. The use of such a cover can result in strawberries being three weeks to a month ahead of the regular fruiting season.

Fuller use of a pyramidal garden, from a landscaping point of view, can be made by turning the top layer into a platform for a bird bath or a sundial, or even into a planting site for a standard or tree rose.

Though everbearing strawberries in the garden can be grown in any type of soil

from sandy to clay loam, there is no doubt that lighter soils are best, since they are easier to work and encourage the formation of a better root system. As with the other June-bearing strawberries, plenty of humus is a must.

Early Spring is the correct time for planting everbearing strawberries. Whether in the regular garden or in the pyramid you set them 12 inches apart. Everbearing strawberries should be grown entirely on the hill system which means that you never allow any runners to form unless you wish to grow a few plants for next year's planting. Of course, in the pyramid garden, lack of space ensures that no runners are ever allowed to form.

Everbearing strawberries, just like the June-bearing kind will start to throw white blossoms during early May, but these should be removed until the first of August. From then on let them flower at will, and around the first of September the out-of-season berries will be ready for picking. Most will be able to enjoy fresh ripe strawberries well into October or even later.

The next season allow the flowers to form at will and you will get a good crop of strawberries in June followed by continu-

ous cropping until late in the Fall.

Everbearing strawberries are best fed with a liquid fertilizer once a month from the time growth starts in the early Spring until the first of September.

Superfection — All strawberry experts seem to be in agreement that Superfection is the best of the everbearing strawberries. It will produce berries 90 days after planting. Berries are round, of firm texture and a dark red color all through. It will ship long distances without losing color or firmness. Bears an abundance of large berries from Spring until frost. 50 to 75 plants will produce enough berries for an average family. Superfection is not only an excellent variety for the home gardener, but is also a good commercial proposition.

Red Rich — Red Rich is a sensational recent introduction in everbearing strawberries, which produces a much larger berry than the older varieties. In fact, if correctly grown, will produce a quart of berries per plant each year. It bears all Summer long, giving luscious honey-sweet strawberries until late in the Fall. Plants are big and strong, with 50 to 75 of them providing enough berries for the average family. Red Rich is a wonderful berry for freezing. It contains so much sugar you can freeze the berries whole and they will not mush when thawed.

Twentieth Century — Twentieth Century comes highly recommended by experiment stations in many States. It rates as superior in size, quality and production. Each year it makes a vigorous growth of good-sized plants. Many bright red berries of fine texture and excellent flavor are produced throughout the season. Twentieth Century is not only a good berry for the home garden, but is also a profit maker for commercial growers.

Chief Bemidji — Here we have a new everbearing strawberry so hardy it will survive temperatures of 40 to 50 degrees below zero. Chief Bemidji survives these Winters with no Winter cover, and rewards you with large beautiful berries, bright scarlet red to the core. It is a big cropper whose berries are high in sugar and low in acid flavor. This Winterproof variety will not only provide you with fine strawberries in June, but also in mid-Summer and again abundantly from September until frost.

A good crop of blackberries in New York state

drying out by placing them in a pail of water, or keeping them covered with a piece of wet burlap. After planting cut back the canes to about twelve inches, at the same time trimming any broken roots. To help the plants become well established and make good growth the first year, be sure to remove any blossoms that appear.

In the colder areas where the temperatures fall to zero or sub-zero frequently, some Winter protection is needed. Pinching back the shoots in the Summer will keep the bushes low so they are less exposed and more protected by snow cover. Taller plants may have to be bent over, the tips of the branches held down by soil, so the snow will be able to cover them.

Bailey — Here is the blackberry considered to be the best variety on the market. Its berries are large, attractive, moderately firm, sub-acid and of good quality. Plants grow tall, are vigorous, hardy and productive. Ripening time is during the last half of July. Bailey is very good for both home gardens and commercial planting.

BLACKBERRIES

The blackberry and related types such as Loganberry and Boysenberry can be easily distinguished from raspberries because the "core" stays in the fruit when it is picked. True blackberries are very tender and will survive only in areas where the Winters are mild, the snowfall heavy, or if given some sort of Winter protection.

The preparation of the soil for blackberries is the same as for raspberries, humus and fertilizer being used at the same rates.

Blackberries must be planted in the Spring, whereas Red raspberries can be planted either in the Fall or early Spring.

Planting — The plants are vigorous growers and so must be set 2½ to 3 feet apart. If planting more than one row, space the rows five to eight feet apart depending on the available space.

Set the plants slightly deeper than the depth at which they grew previously, making sure when packing the soil around them not to break off the young growing shoots. During planting keep the roots from

Blackberries are not nearly as hardy as raspberries

22

GOOSEBERRIES

Like all other native plants of North America gooseberries are extremely easy to grow, in fact they have been found growing wild almost to the Arctic circle.

If properly cared for, young plants set in permanent locations in the garden need not be replanted for many years. When allowed to ripen on the vines, the berries make particularly fine eating as fresh fruit, and most people are aware of the fine pies, jams and other preserves made from this widely known but little grown fruit.

spells, causing the leaves to fall prematurely and the fruits to scald in the sun. In preparing the soil for gooseberries, it must be kept in mind that they are heavy feeders. Dig humus into the soil at the rate of 6 to 8 bushels per hundred square feet. For really poor soils increase the amount of humus to 10 to 12 bushels per 100 square feet. Any of the materials mentioned as good for mulching purposes also make good humus materials. At the same time, work into the soil a complete fertilizer at the rate of 4 pounds per 100 feet.

To give ample room for cultivation and mulching, set the plants 4 feet apart in the row and, if you are planting more than one row, space the rows 6 feet. Commercial plantings are often set as much as 10 feet apart. Make sure the bushes are set somewhat deeper than they stood in the nursery. Then tramp the soil well about them. If the plants are of a variety that does not branch naturally, set them so the lowest branch starts just below the surface of the soil. This will prevent the development of a tree type of plant.

Gooseberries are easy to grow

The best time to prune gooseberries is in the early Winter, when you remove all wood more than three years old. Also cut off all branches that touch the ground.

Shape the gooseberry bush so that you retain five or six vigorous shoots so as to make an open head, making it easier to pick fruit later on.

Soil preparation — For most other small fruits a loam or sandy loam soil is usually the best, but for gooseberries, well-drained, heavy clay loams are the most suitable. The gooseberry is a moisture-loving plant and heavy clay loams not only provide the moisture but also keep the roots cool. In very light sandy soil conditions gooseberries suffer greatly in hot, dry

Planting — Gooseberries are best planted in the Fall because their buds usually start to grow early in the Spring before the ground is workable. Fall planting is helped by the fact the leaves drop so early that September planting is possible, thus giving the bushes a chance to become well established before the heavy frost arrives, in November and early December.

Strong, well-rooted one year plants are the best kind to buy. Do not be persuaded to buy 2 year or older bushes, as apart from being more expensive they are not easily moved.

Just before planting, the bushes should be cut back to 6 inches to 12 inches depending on the vigor. At the same time trim off any broken roots.

Care and Feeding — During July and early August, when the sun heats the surface of the soil to a very high temperature, each bush should be surrounded with a mulch 2 to 3 inches deep, extending from the trunk of the bush to well beyond the outer spread of the branches.

In October the mulch can be dug into the soil to add to the existing supply of humus. Materials processed from sewage, peat moss, well-rotted barnyard manure, discarded mushroom manure and compost all may be used as a mulch with good results.

In addition to digging in the mulch each Fall to increase the supply of humus, it is advisable to feed the gooseberries as soon as the ground is workable in the early Spring with a complete fertilizer. The first

Poorman — This variety is especially noteworthy because of its vigor and the heavy crop it produces. The bushes produce numerous new shoots. Berries are large and green colored at first, later changing to an attractive red. Flesh is tender, juicy, of good quality and quite sweet when ripe.

Pixwell is a new variety and considered the best on the market today. It is a particularly heavy bearer with berries which turn to a delightful pinkish red. The easily picked fruit is borne the first year after planting.

year after planting, use a small handful per bush, older bushes will require double this amount. Scatter it around the outer spread of the branches and gently work it into the soil with a garden rake.

When raking, make sure the rake does not penetrate too deeply as the roots of the gooseberry grow near the surface. The same applies when cultivating around the bushes to keep the weeds in check. About the middle of June, give the bushes a final shallow, but thorough cultivation, then apply the mulch as recommended before. This should eliminate the need for cultivation the rest of the season.

Pruning — Gooseberries produce most of their fruit on spurs on the older branches, but some fruit is produced on year old wood. Bushes normally make much more wood than is desirable, so fairly heavy pruning is necessary. A good rule of thumb to follow is to remove all wood more than three years old and the best time to do it is in the Fall or Winter.

In pruning we try to shape the bush by leaving five or six of the strongest shoots growing toward the outside of the bush. The weakest young shoots should be cut off at the soil level. As the bushes grow older and bigger allow new shoots to replace the older ones. Cut back the side shoots from the older branches or cut them out altogether to help maintain an open head. This has the added advantage of making it easier to pick the fruit yet leaving enough foliage to protect the fruit from being scalded by the sun.

Cut back bushes 6 to 12 inches just before planting

Red Jacket — This variety is the largest and has the highest quality of all gooseberries. The fascinating, red-skinned fruit is carried upon vigorous sturdy bushes. Red Jacket is extremely easy to grow, hardy and productive.

Downing is the most popular of all the green gooseberries. Excellent, large green fruits appear in quantity the first year after planting. Bushes are very hardy.

Captivator — This has been the most impressive of the thornless varieties to date. Bushes have a fine upright habit, and are vigorous and hardy. The only thorns to be found on the bush are a few at the base of some of the shoots, but these certainly are not troublesome. Berries are about the same size as Poorman, have thick skins, are pear-shaped and turn red when ripe.

THORNLESS BOYSENBERRY

It combines all the delicious sweet flavors of its blackberry, loganberry and raspberry ancestors. Some of the huge berries have measured up to 2 inches in length, sixty of the berries easily filling a quart box. Boysenberries are ripe for four to six weeks beginning in early July. Bushes start to bear fruit about 14 months after planting. The canes are as smooth as velvet and fruit is produced 10 days to two weeks earlier than the common boysenberry. It is certainly a pleasure to pick the large juicy berries without scratching your hands.

BLACK & RED CURRANTS

Black and red currants are among the hardiest of the small fruit plants having been grown far to the north of Canada.

The fruit makes very nutritious jams and jellies, in particular black currants have a very high vitamin C content.

Currants thrive in rich, cool well-drained soils and are best located on northern slopes. Avoid sandy soils as their roots grow close to the surface and so will suffer during hot Summer months. The plants are moisture-loving but must not be set in places where water stands for any length of time.

Currants burst into bloom very early in the Spring and so should not be planted in known frost pockets. Frost pockets usually form in bottoms of hollows or valleys.

Preparation of soil — A thorough preparation of the soil is necessary before setting currants out in the garden. Like gooseberries they are a fairly permanent crop, and are heavy feeders, therefore the soil should receive plenty of humus and fertilizer a week or so before planting is to take place. For average garden soils apply the humus at the rate of six to eight bushels per hundred square feet, stepping this up to 10 to 12 bushels in poor sub-division soils. At the same time, spread over the planting bed a complete fertilizer at the rate of 4 pounds per 100 square feet. The top 6 to 8 inches of soil, the humus and the fertilizer should then be thoroughly mixed together.

Planting — The most advisable way of obtaining the plants is to buy them from a reliable nursery. Strong, well-rooted one-year-old plants are the best, they are not only less expensive, but take root more easily and suffer less set-back from transplanting than do two-year-old plants. Currant bushes should be planted in 4 foot squares, allowing 6 feet between plants— the square permits easier cultivation. Plants

must be set slightly deeper than the depth at which they were growing in the nursery, and the soil should be firmed well around the roots at planting.

Fall planting is preferred for currants because they drop their leaves early in the Fall and start growth early in the Spring. However early Spring planting should normally be satisfactory.

The ardent home gardener can very easily propagate his own plants from both red and black currant bushes. During October take cuttings from the new or current season wood. Each cutting to be six to eight inches long, with the bottom cut just below a bud, and the top cut one-half an inch above a bud. Next, set the cuttings six inches apart in well-drained soil, so that one or two buds extend out of the soil, then mulch with two or three inches of straw or hay. The next Fall, the plants will be large enough to set out in the garden.

Care of bushes — In cultivating currants you have to keep in mind that they are surface rooters and so hoeing must be extremely shallow. It is probably best to cultivate or hoe until early in June and then surround the bushes with a mulch of hay, straw, peat moss or other humus material, 2 to 3 inches deep.

Each Spring a half a pound of complete fertilizer should be applied to mature plants covering the area under the branches and extending a foot or so beyond their outer spread. For young plants one or two years old, a large handful of fertilizer will be the right amount to apply.

Red lake currants are a pleasure to pick

With good soil conditions, a mature red currant bush should yield from five to six quarts a year

Pruning — Pruning of currants should be completed in late Winter or the very early Spring, when the plants are dormant.

Pruning black currants — Black currants produce the best fruit on one year old wood and so it is good policy not to allow the bushes to retain a large number of thick, black older branches. Just as soon as these start to form, they should be removed. Plan to keep a total of about 10 to 12 shoots per mature bush, with at least half of these being one-year-old shoots. Ruthlessly cut out any wood that is older than two years.

Consort — This is a complete rust resistant variety, whose fruits are large and the yield is very good. Bushes are strong growers and very easy to transplant. It is an ideal variety for the small home garden.

Kerry — There is no doubt that Kerry is one of the very best black currants grown. Fruits are extra large and the bushes very productive and hardy.

Magnus is a new, large and early black currant. Clusters are medium in size but the fruits are of good size and quality.

Pruning red currants — Red currants are treated like gooseberries as most of their fruit is produced on spurs on the two and three-year-old branches. You will need to regulate the pruning so that each bush will contain three or four shoots each of three-, two- and one-year-old wood, making sure to remove branches older than three years.

Provided soil conditions are good, a mature black or red currant bush should yield from five to six quarts of fruit per year. The bushes will remain productive for at least eight to ten years provided correct pruning as recommended above is carried out.

Red Lake — This is the best variety to grow both in the home garden and in commercial planting. The clear scarlet red berries unusually large in size and of superior quality, are borne on long clusters. Bushes are very vigorous, upright, productive and hardy. In fruit and plant characteristics, the Red Lake is much superior to any red currant yet developed. Six bushes will give the average family enough fruit for making pies, jams or jellies. You will discover that it can be planted well in either Spring or Fall.

26

ALL ABOUT GRAPES

A grape vine not only makes a fine climbing vine, but it also can provide tasty fruit for the table. Of course in the really colder parts of North America where sub-zero temperatures are frequent it is not possible to grow grapes because they are not hardy enough, but in the warmer parts a grape vine is a useful addition to the garden.

Grapes can be treated like a climbing rose or any other vine and trained to grow along a fence, a wall, over an arbor or up the side of a porch.

Grapes will grow in a wider variety of soil conditions and climate than any other fruit. They are extremely easy to care for and a single vine will bear ten pounds or more of delicious fruit. By making a selection of varieties it is possible to have ripe grapes in the garden from the last week in August until the middle of October, depending on the date of the first hard frost in the area.

Seibel is a French hybrid grape for the home garden

Portland, early-ripening white grape

Planting — Planting time is just as soon as the soil is workable in the early Spring. In preparing to plant, first dig a planting hole two feet square and two feet deep. Replace the soil removed with a soil mixture consisting of two parts good top-soil and one part humus. To each bushel of this mixture, add a large handful of complete fertilizer. A complete fertilizer is one containing balanced amounts of nitrogen, phosphorus and potash.

Set the vines at the same level as they were in the nursery by checking the soil line which can be easily seen on the trunk of the vine. Spread the fibrous roots to all sides of the planting hole. Then add three or four inches of soil and firm it well around the roots. It won't hurt to gently firm the soil with your feet. Once the planting hole is half full, fill it up with water and let it drain away before filling in the remainder of the soil.

Disease and insect pests — Mildew, a fungus disease, and leaf hoppers, an insect pest, are the only disease and insect problems usually encountered in grape vines.

Even these are mainly dependent on weather conditions. Mildew attacks only in seasons when there has been an extra heavy rainfall. Leaf hoppers become a pest when the weather is extra hot and dry. Both can be kept under control, together with any other blight or insect that might take a liking to the vines, by spraying or dusting the grape vines every ten days with one of the all-purpose insecticides and fungicides. Dusting or spraying should stop at least three weeks before the fruit is ripe.

Pruning — Success in growing grapes and getting them to fruit well really depends on correct pruning. Like any other job around the garden or farm, you must have good tools. Here the most important tool is a good pair of pruners. There are two main types on the market.

One has a steel blade cutting down on to a brass plate. The blade, the spring and the brass plate are all replaceable. This type of pruner does less damage and cuts more easily than the other type.

Grape vines should be pruned every year during January or February. You cannot

27

delay the pruning into March as you would with roses because the sap starts to rise in the grape vines very early and late pruning will seriously affect the health of the vine.

Vines are pruned every year to reduce the amount of wood, to limit the amount of foliage, and to keep the vine off the ground. This exposes the fruit to much needed light, sunshine and air, and also permits a more thorough spraying or dusting.

It is often hard for the home gardener to be ruthless, but in the case of the grape vine and with many other shrubs and trees that is exactly what he has to be.

Grapes are borne on wood stalks produced the previous season; the wood will be brown, reddish brown or gray depending on the variety. Except for the main trunk it is useless to keep any unnecessary wood over a year in age. In pruning we aim to achieve a balance between wood and fruit production. Where the balance is correct the vines produce a good crop of large-clustered bunches of grapes and enough wood for sturdy arms the following season.

A big mistake is to prune too lightly thus making the vines produce too much wood and a large number of small clusters of grapes. It is also possible to prune too heavily.

There are various systems of pruning a grape vine along a wall, fence or special wires. The most common system is called the Kniffen. With this system the central trunk rises straight up from the ground, the arms of new budding wood being trained along wires at right angles to the trunk.

A normally vigorous vine should be pruned to 40 buds. The best canes to use for arms are those about the thickness of a pencil and having plump buds. As the most productive buds on the cane are usually the third to the ninth, the 40 buds should be left on four ten-bud arms rather than on several short ones.

When pruning grape vines, it is essential to stimulate new growth for the central trunk every year — the development of old wood for the arms must be avoided.

In choosing a new arm select a strong healthy piece of new wood originating as close as possible to the central trunk. At the same time choose another healthy piece of new wood to make a spur, also as close as possible to the central trunk. By spurring we mean leaving a piece of new wood about three to four inches in length having two buds. From one or both of these buds

will grow new wood for next year's arm. All other growth, except the new arm and the spur, is removed. The usual practice is

to have four to six of these arms per vine. If the growth is strong and vigorous leave five or six buds per arm.

Himrod will withstand temperatures of 20° below zero without harm

Care of grape vines

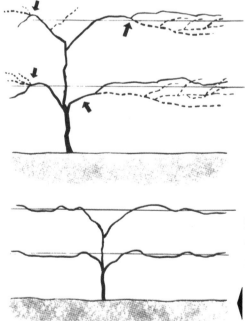

Prune grapes in winter. They start to grow very early in the Spring when you will want to do other jobs. Spring pruning and subsequent bleeding is not harmful, but young buds are liable to be damaged in the process.

Grapes are easy to prune if trained as sketched. Prune in four cuts. Each bud on remaining stem will produce one or two clusters of grapes. Leave only 40 to 60 buds on a vine for large bunches and best quality grapes.

White Grapes

The Niagara is the most popular white grape

Himrod — Is a new superior seedless grape developed by plant breeders at the New York State Experiment Station and is the product of years of testing and research. This great new grape produces abundant, rich golden yellow berries, hanging in loose clusters which invite you to enjoy the sweet delicious wine-like flavor. Each amber berry can be eaten whole like California grapes because there are no seeds. Vines are big producers and the fruit is ripe about the middle of September. Himrod is easy to grow, free from disease and very vigorous. There is no need to worry about its hardiness in most sections because the vines withstand temperatures of 20 degrees below zero without harm.

Niagara — Here is the most popular and best known white grape. Most years it ripens about the last week in September, although if you happen to get a hot spell earlier in the month it can ripen around the 18th to the 20th. Vines produce large clusters of tangy, yellowish-green grapes of dessert quality. These are very sweet tasting and make fine jams and jellies. Hardiness is not a problem.

Seibel — was developed in France, and its berries are colored a beautiful golden yellow. This is a good grape for the home garden because of its excellent dessert qualities and early ripening habit. Very often 2-year old vines will start to bear fruit. Ripening time is about September 15th. The grapes have crisp texture and the good eating quality makes this new French hybrid a fine variety.

Golden Muscat (California type grape) One of the finest grapes ever developed. Berries are sweeter, larger, and more luscious than many of the wonderful "old country sweet grapes" made famous by the European vineyards. Vines are vigorous, hardy and extremely productive. Bunches are very large, and carry big oval golden berries of the highest quality. The flesh of the berries is juicy, tender, with a wonderful Muscat flavor, excellent for eating or for making jelly or juice. Grapes are ripe around the 5th to the 10th of October. This

**Golden Muscat possesses the rich color and fine aroma of the
European muscat grape**

may be a little late in some areas, and before you buy, it is advisable to check the
average date of the first killing frost in
your area. If this occurs during the first
week of October then it is not wise to plant
Golden muscat.

Portland — This is the variety to plant
in locations where a hard frost comes early
in the season. Portland holds first place
as the early white variety and ripens during
the first week of September. Attractive full
clusters of the largest white grapes are produced in quantity. Berries are big, firm,
sweet and extra juicy. Vines are good croppers, hardy, healthy and will grow well
in most locations.

Red Grapes

Caco — A fine new grape which is pro-
ving to be a great favorite in the home
garden. The large, wine-red bunches of
sweet, palatable fruit make this the most
beautiful of the hardy grapes. Ripening
time is towards the end of September. Berries are very large and sweet. This is a
fine variety for growing over a trellis.

Red grapes make delicious eating

Stark Delicious (Girard) — An extra fine red grape produced on large bunches. The medium sized berries attain top flavor when left on the vine until deep crimson. This variety is a strong grower and a fine pollinizer. Ripening time in most areas is around the middle of September, although it can be earlier, depending on the season. Starts to bear when very young, often on one-year vines. An excellent variety for eating fresh or for making jelly or juice.

Lindley — One of the finest red grapes for home use. A heavy producer of large, sweet, juicy and firm red fruit. It is doubtful if there is a better red variety for eating as fresh grapes from the vine.

Black Grapes

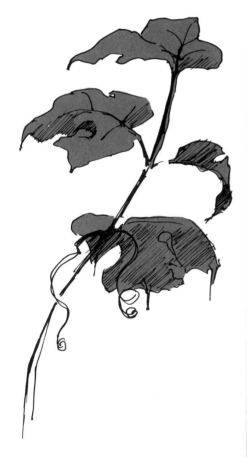

Concord is excellent for eating and for grape juice

Fredonia is the earliest good black grape, ripening about the middle of September. Berries are very large, hang well to the bunch, are firm and juicy and of fine flavor. Vines are vigorous and productive with medium size very compact bunches or clusters. This is a good variety for commercial use, because the bunches keep their vine-fresh firmness and fresh appearance for days after picking.

Van Buren, the earliest grape to ripen

Concord is the most widely planted of all grapes

Steuben — This beautiful variety has an exquisite flavor and is tender and sweet. Clusters are huge, perfectly formed and long and slender in shape. The grapes keep well in storage and the ripening date is around the 1st of October. Vines are very hardy and have produced full crops following 20 degrees below zero temperatures. No spraying or dusting is necessary as it is absolutely free from mildew and rot. Under good storage conditions the grapes will keep until Christmas.

Van Buren — A deliciously flavored new hardy blue grape, which should be a great favorite in the home garden and in vineyards which supply roadside and local markets. It resembles Concord, but is much sweeter and very juicy. Ripening time is the last week in August or the first in September. Vines are hardy, vigorous and heavy producers. Van Buren is an excellent table grape.

Concord—There is absolutely no doubt that Concord is the most widely planted of all grapes. Concord produces the biggest yields and is hardy in most localities. The vines are not the slightest bit particular about the type of soil in which they are planted. Handsome bunches of large luscious blue-black fruits are produced each year. The skin of the berries is tender but firm and the flesh is juicy and sweet. Fruits are unexcelled for wines, jams, jellies and for table use.

A fine crop of sweet juicy Concord grapes

A large fine quality bunch

Steuben has an exquisite flavor

33

MUSKMELONS OR CANTALOUPES

Burpee Hybrid is a fine cantaloupe

fertilizer; apply at the rate of 4 pounds per 100 square feet. Whatever you do, avoid using a high nitrogen fertilizer such as used on lawns because the nitrogen will produce rank growth of the vines and little if any melons.

Planting — The best way of handling melons is to plant three or four seeds in 3-inch peat pots, clay pots or veneer plant bands about the first week in May. The peat pots are the best containers to use because the plants can be set in the garden still in the pot around the first of June when soil and air temperatures have really warmed up. Plants should be set four feet apart each way.

Seeds can be planted directly in the garden where they are to grow, but are very tempting to birds and insects just after sprouting. Seed sown directly in the garden should be set around the middle of May and then covered with a small plastic container sold especially for the purpose. When the melon plants grow through the ground, the cover will not only protect them from birds and insects, but will have heated the soil and the air sufficiently for the melons

Muskmelons require the same care and growing conditions as cucumbers, pumpkins and squash. They are all vigorous growers and require a fair amount of space, which can create a problem in the smaller home garden. Often this can be overcome by growing the muskmelons on a fence instead of allowing the vines to lie on the ground.

Muskmelons require a warm soil and a temperature of 70 to 80 degrees before they start growing well.

Preparation of soil — Melons demand an exceedingly rich soil which contains large amounts of humus and fertilizer. In ordinary garden soils you will need six to eight bushels of humus per hundred square feet. In the average poor sub-division soil, 10 to 12 bushels of humus will be needed. Well-rotted barnyard manure, discarded mushroom manure, or peat moss are the best forms of humus to use. Use a complete

Muskmelons require a fair amount of space

34

to develop. Germination requires four to ten days at a temperature of 65 to 75 degrees. At lower temperatures the seed may rot or fail to germinate.

To really enjoy a muskmelon, the fruit should be allowed to fully ripen on the vine. Fruits will be ripe when the stem attached to the melon will slip from it with a slight touch of the thumb. If the stem does not slip off easily, the melon is not ripe and should remain on the vine.

Burpee Hybrid — This is an orange-fleshed cantaloupe or muskmelon which takes 82 days from the time the seed is sown until the first fruit can be picked. It is a true first generation F1 hybrid noted for its quality and flavor. Fruits are heavily netted, ribbed, round to slightly oval in shape. They have an average weight of around 4½ pounds, and average seven inches long and six inches across. Flesh is deep orange, thick, firm, juicy, sweet and the seed cavity is very small.

Honey Rock (special strain)—Be sure and buy the "special strain" which has great resistance to the fusarium wilt. In some catalogs you will find this also listed as Sugar Rock. It takes 85 days from the time the seed is sown until the fruits are ready for picking. The attractive, well netted fruits are slightly more oval than the original strain of Honey Rock. The thick, deeply colored salmon flesh is deliciously sweet, with a fine smooth texture. Here is a variety whose vigorous, dark green vines are resistant to disease, and stand up well under adverse growing conditions. Fruits are medium in size, averaging 5½ inches in diameter, and weigh about 3 pounds each.

Muskmelons are ripe when the stem attached to the melon will slip from it with a slight touch of the thumb

Sugar Salmon is the earliest good quality melon, taking just 70 to 75 days from sowing to fruiting. The flesh is a rich salmon in color and of a sweet and delicate texture. Sugar Salmon ripens a heavy crop of well netted high quality fruits early in the season.

Pennsweet — This is one of the sweetest of all melons. It is highly suitable for planting in short season northern areas. Very early, small sized fruits, notable for a thick, sweet yellow flesh, with small seed cavity are produced in abundance. It takes 70 days from seeding until fruiting.

Far North — The small melons of this variety mature earlier than any other kind. They are of excellent quality and are the only ones which will mature correctly in many northern areas. Far North is recommended for home garden use only. The fruits are ripe 64 days after the seed is sown.

Harper Hybrid — Here is an F1 hybrid which has shown marked resistance to fusarium wilt. It will yield good crops of moderate size melons of excellent flavor. Fruits are round, well netted with a creamy white skin. The seed cavity is quite small, and flesh is thick and salmon colored. Harper Hybrid is a good variety to grow commercially.

35

Warm Climate Melons

This type of melon is grown extensively in California for local markets, distant shipping and in the home garden. They are late maturing, so need a long season to produce their crop of delicious melons. It is possible to beat the season by starting the melons off indoors and then moving them outdoors around the first of June. About the middle of September, the vines could be covered with a cold frame to protect the exotic, delicious fruits.

Golden Beauty Casaba — It takes 120 days from the time the seed is sown until the fruits start to ripen. They are globular in shape, 6 to 8 inches in diameter and have a golden yellow tough wrinkled skin. The sweet flesh is very thick, white and juicy. They will keep in good condition for several months.

Honeydew—These green fleshed melons take 110 days from seeding until the fruit ripens. They have a broad oval shape and measure 7 to 8 inches in length and six inches in diameter. The skin is smooth and ivory colored, and the flesh is very sweet, juicy and a pale emerald green in color. Honeydew is also a good keeper.

Muskmelons require the same care and growing conditions as cucumbers, pumpkins and squash

WATERMELONS

Like muskmelons, watermelons should be started indoors about the first of May in peat pots and then moved outdoors. Set the pots containing the seedling in the garden at the beginning of June. Watermelons also like the soil to contain plenty of humus and fertilizer. Since the vines are vigorous growers and cover a lot of ground, they have to be planted 8 feet apart.

A light sandy loam is definitely the best kind of soil for melons of any kind. In most northern areas, the problem will be to plant varieties which will mature before the vines can be cut down by frost. New Hampshire or Burpee's Fordhook F1 Hybrid are probably the best varieties to grow in such circumstances.

New Hampshire Midget — 70 days for its fruits to ripen after the seed is sown. Home gardeners in the north will certainly appreciate its extreme earliness. Fruits are quite a bit smaller than the ordinary watermelon, and are about as big as a muskmelon or cantaloupe. They will average 7 inches long and 6 inches in diameter, and weigh about six pounds. Skin is striped dark green on light green, the rind is thin, and flesh is strawberry red, solid and sweet. Vines are small, thus making them ideal for the home garden. New Hampshire Midget is a vigorous and heavy yielding variety.

Burpee's Fordhook F1 Hybrid
Fruits of this fine variety are a dark glossy green in color, nearly round and weighs from 12 to 14 pounds. It is an outstanding family-size melon for the home garden. Melons which ripen 74 days after sowing the seed, have bright red flesh with a moderate number of small seeds. The vines are early and prolific producers.

Burpee's F1 Hybrid Seedless — This is a Tri-X hybrid grown by Burpee having oval fruits averaging 10 to 15 pounds or larger, with solid bright red flesh of the sweetest flavor. It is true there are no seeds, but you will find scattered through the flesh tiny soft white seed coats which are completely edible and practically unnoticeable.

The green striped melons are borne on healthy vigorous vines which resist disease. Seedless watermelons will not set fruits unless pollinated by normal watermelons planted nearby. It is a good plan to have one hill of New Hampshire Midget or Burpee's Fordhook F1 Hybrid to every two or three hills of Burpee's F1 Hybrid Seedless.

Tri-X Hybrids like to have the soil a little warmer. The soil temperature required to germinate these seeds is slightly higher than for seeded watermelons. The optimum soil temperature is about 85°, so if you are going to plant Tri-X seed directly in your garden, you will not be able to rush the season too much.

If you have a long melon-growing season, direct seeding in the garden is probably the method you should use. However, farther north with shorter growing seasons, you can either start the seed indoors as recommended for cantaloupes or muskmelons, or use a cold frame.

After the plants start to grow well, cultivation should be shallow to avoid root damage. Three or four cultivations are usually adequate. Remember that melon roots are shallow growing and they will extend farther than the vines. Also, damaged roots will mean a much reduced yield.

Picking a ripened watermelon is an art. With normal varieties there is no doubt that care should be exercised, but in seedless varieties, even more training is required in learning to judge the maturity of the fruits. Seedless melons tend to be sweet even when picked a little too early. Here are some points to serve as a guide:

1. Count the number of days from blooming period to ripeness. Among early planting, 40 days from blooming to fruit is about the time. Later plantings require 30 days, and late sets take about 24 days.

2. The tendril next to fruit begins withering as melon ripens. About one third of the tendril withered is a good indication.

3. When the bottom portion of the melon shows yellowness and toughening.

4. The roughening of rind on the bottom side indicates ripeness.

5. A glossy surface of the melon.

6. Dull sounds from tapping or snapping indicates ripeness, but the usual sounding for melons does not hold with seedless fruit.

The ability to pick ripe melons depends upon several features taken together. Any one point cannot be used to the exclusion of all the others. After experience, very few mistakes will be made in picking ripe melons.

Burpee's Fordhook hybrid watermelon is early and productive

RHUBARB

Picking a ripened watermelon is an art

Rhubarb, while officially classed as a vegetable, always seems to be more of a fruit. In any case, it is a perennial which is best grown from plants rather than seeds.

It is worth growing in the average home garden, because once it starts producing it will go on for a number of years. Planting time is in the early Spring, just as soon as the soil is workable.

The soil for rhubarb should be rich and well drained. Work into it before planting, a quantity of humus at the rate of 8 to 10 bushels per 100 square feet together with a complete fertilizer at the rate of 4 pounds per 100 square feet. Set the roots six inches deep and be sure to firm the earth well around the roots. Best way of doing this is to tramp the earth down with both feet using full weight. Set the plants four feet apart in the row and make the rows five feet apart. Rhubarb must be planted in a location where it is easy to control the growth of weeds and grass.

No rhubarb should be pulled the first year after planting. This is in order to give the roots a chance to become well established. Notice we said "pull" and not "cut". Rhubarb should never be cut with a knife. You pull it because the whole stalk is usable. Many persons are mistaken in thinking that rhubarb is only usable in the early Spring. On the contrary, the stalks make just as good eating when young and vigorous in the Summer.

When buying plants be sure you get them from a reliable nursery, and not from a neighbour's patch. This will materially lessen the chance of getting old and probably diseased stock. Once these plants are infected by crown rot, there is not much you can do about it except to get clean plants from a reliable nursery and set them out in a part of the garden where you have not grown rhubarb before.

Home gardeners with larger gardens can dig some two- or three-year-old plants in the late Fall, leave them out on the top of the ground to freeze solidly. In January, they can be brought indoors and set in a barrel or deep box on a bed of straw and forced in the basement. It will not be long before some choice rhubarb for a Winter dessert treat can be pulled.

Rhubarb can be easily forced indoors

FRUIT TREES

FRUIT TREES

Fruit trees reward you with beauty as well as fruit

They will not only provide the garden with delicious tasting fruits, but you also get two or three weeks of exquisite bloom from them early in the garden season.

Planting — In some advertisements you will see fruit trees listed as "bearing age." Don't be fooled by this. There is absolutely no advantage to planting such trees and in most cases you won't get as good results as if you'd planted trees of the recommended age.

Best planting age for fruit trees

Apple	1 or 2 years
Peach	1 year
Cherry	1 or 2 years
Plum	2 years
Pears	2 years

How to plant — Fruit trees can be planted with success in either the Spring or Fall. To ensure fruit trees getting off to a good start, the planting hole should be a good size one. A hole 2 feet wide and 2 feet deep is usually the most satisfactory. True enough, you could get away with a hole 15 inches deep and 15 inches across, but the extra depth and width means that the tree will have lots of nourishment not only immediately available, but for several years to come.

Any earth removed from the hole should be discarded in favour of a correctly prepared planting mixture. Commercially prepared soil mixtures can be bought from the nursery or garden center where you purchased your fruit trees or they are available from hardware, department stores, and other places where garden supplies are sold.

It's a good plan, if possible, to have the planting holes dug before you go out to the nursery to pick up your trees. As soon as you arrive home, be sure to get them in the ground. More trees and other nursery stock are killed each year because the stock dries

Most gardeners would like to have one or two fruit trees; some are even ambitious to have an orchard. In either case fruit trees are a challenge. They reward a little care handsomely — with beauty and fruit.

With fruit trees we emphasize again, think before you plant. If you have a small lot or back yard then your choice should be dwarf trees. With these you can have a bigger variety of different fruits. You must also consider whether you want late or early bearing varieties.

Before buying any variety of fruit tree be sure to check with your nurseryman for what grows best in your locality.

There aren't many gardens where there is room to grow a standard size apple tree. For instance, a mature Northern Spy apple tree will cover a thousand square feet of space. However, the standard varieties of plums, pears, cherries, peaches and apricots can add a great deal of beauty to the garden, and at the same time won't take up too much room.

out too much before planting. The roots should be kept covered with a piece of wet burlap or some other material until time to set the trees in the hole.

A small mound of soil should be built up in the bottom of the hole on which to place the tree. This is done to eliminate possible air pockets which in turn would allow the roots to dry out, and in many cases kill the tree. Just before placing the tree in the hole, it should be examined for any damaged or broken roots and these should be removed with a sharp knife or pruning shears. The roots should be spread out evenly to all sides of the hole and then 3 or 4 inches of soil added and then firmed well around the roots. As the soil is filled in, jiggle the tree a little so that all the roots will make contact with the soil. Keep on adding and firming the soil until the hole is half full. Next, fill the hole with water and let this drain away before filling in the remainder of the soil and firming it.

It's true that you could get away without staking most fruit trees, but experience has shown that a stake can be very valuable in keeping the trees straight and upright until

A dwarf or semi-dwarf apple tree is best for the garden

Fruit trees are a challenge

they have had a chance to form roots and so keep themselves in line. Stakes should be put in place before the earth is filled in around the roots. If you try to put a stake in place after the hole has been filled in, you'll very often do quite a bit of damage to the roots.

Apple trees

Close is by far the earliest apple to ripen and is an annual bearer of good crops. The apples average 2½ inches in diameter and up and are wonderful for cooking. "Close" is a good shipper and does not bruise easily. The fruit is an attractive striped red with snow white flesh which is crisp and fine

textured. The trees grow vigorously and produce quantities of fine fruit.

Early MacIntosh — Don't confuse this with the regular Winter MacIntosh. However it resembles its MacIntosh parent with its handsome red colour and uniform round shape. For the home orchard or commercial use this is an ideal early variety to plant. Trees are vigorous growers, hardy and productive. It tends to bear fruit every other year, although early thinning will often force the trees to fruit annually. Early MacIntosh comes into bearing at an early age, and the flesh is white, tender and juicy with a fine flavour.

Wealthy — This variety of apple un-

A highly colored summer apple with extra good quality

are often produced the first year after planting. Colour is a glowing sunny yellow, sometimes blushed with rose. Fruits are extra large and often measure 4 inches or more in diameter. The flavour is sweet and delicious touched with a faint trace of spicy acidity. In areas close to Chicago and Detroit the fruit is ready for picking early in October. It is always a good, solid, crisp, juicy late keeper. Makes fine apple sauce and mouth-watering pies, and is one of the best apples for eating.

Red Delicious is one of the most popular apples grown today, either in the home garden or in commercial orchards. It is an extra large apple, fine solid red in colour, with cream-coloured flesh. There have been individual fruits of this variety which measured $4\frac{1}{2}$ inches in length and 4 inches in diameter. It will be ready for picking about the first of October in most areas adjacent to Chicago and Detroit. Red Delicious has fine keeping qualities, and stays crisp and juicy until the beginning of Spring. It is acclaimed everywhere as one of the very best eating apples, owing to its very mild and almost sweet flavour. Trees grow vig-

doubtedly has the best quality of all the Summer apples. Fruits are very beautiful, moderate in size and coloured a brilliant red. Wealthy trees are extremely hardy and can be widely planted in cold climates. The trees start to produce apples at a very early age, and bear heavily. Juice is refreshing and wine-like. Wealthy apples are excellent cookers and make extremely good eating.

Yellow or Golden Delicious is without a doubt the best yellow apple in the world. On dwarf trees, big luscious golden apples

Apple trees can be used as lawn specimen trees

Flowering crab apples are one of the hardiest flowering trees

orously, producing quantities of fruit at an early age. The hardiness of the Red Delicious has never been questioned.

Cortland is a cross between MacIntosh and Ben Davis, and exhibits the best qualities of both. It's a good dessert apple maturing later than MacIntosh. Trees are strong growers and very hardy. Fruits are red, extra large and round. Cortland apples are always excellent keepers.

MacIntosh Red has been one of the top rated and most popular apples ever since it was found growing in Eastern Ontario almost a century ago. This is a tender, juicy, winter apple with a peculiar fragrance that makes it popular everywhere. Colour is a beautiful crimson red and the flesh is

crisp, delicate and almost snow white. Trees are extremely long lived, very hardy, strong spreading growers which come into bearing when they are very young. Fruits are large and very juicy, the trees being annual and prolific bearers. The apples are excellent for eating, cooking, drying and for making cider.

Northern Spy — For after-Christmas eating, there is no apple to touch the distinctive and pleasing flavour of a Northern Spy apple. Flesh is crisp, firm, juicy, and the fruits are equally good for eating or cooking. The apples are large in size and solid red in colour. The trees are extremely hardy, long lived, vigorous and very productive. In addition to being excellent eating and cooking apples, they also make

first-class cider.

Rhode Island Greening is unsurpassed as a cooking apple and also is very good for eating. It's a good keeper, but keeps better if picked early. This Greening is a beautiful yellow colour when ripe and bears heavy crops which start when the trees are very young.

Dolgo Crab Apple — Crab apple jelly is a favourite with nearly everyone and the Dolgo Crab Apple produces masses of bright red fruit which are unsurpassed for jelly.

Stark Florence Crab is another extremely valuable red variety of crab apple. Trees are heavy producers of crimson red crab apples of good size, which are unexcelled for jelly, preserves, jams and pickles. You will find the trees dwarf in size, and together with the pink blooms and ruby red fruits, they make one of the best trees for ornamental planting in the lawn. Some trees have been known to produce half a bushel of fruit when only two years old.

Starkrimson Delicious Apple — The semi-dwarf which reaches two thirds the size of a standard apple tree in growth and won't overrun the average sized garden. The smaller stature of the tree is a boon to gardeners as it facilitates pruning.

One of the world's largest apple growers has said that it is a great apple on a great tree and that it produces fruit in eighteen months.

A horticulturist expert is on record as having praised its quality and colour, its

Dwarf trees for the beginner

attractiveness (making it easier to sell) and its characteristic of attaining its high colour early, thus enabling it to be picked while juicy and crisp.

Why is Starkrimson so different to other apples? First of all, its colour is a brilliant glossy red which on the usual Delicious harvesting date grades 100 percent Extra Fancy for colour.

Secondly, it's a Fruit-Spur Type tree producing fruit-bearing spurs which cover the limbs down to and sometimes even on the trunk.

Most fruits on regular apple trees are borne on fruit spurs which are short, fat growth along the limbs of bearing age trees. Starkrimson has a completely different habit of growth from regular trees. The main difference is the more abundant production of strong fruit spurs which are well distributed throughout the trees. The fruit spurs are blunt, not sharp. All fruit spur buds are round and fat as contrasted to the long, sharp leaf buds. The fruit spurs form at a much younger age than on any other type of apple tree. This brings Starkrimson into younger and heavier production and also gives better annual bearing, since there are always a number of spurs resting during each growing season to produce next year's crop.

Tests in many sections of North America have proved that Starkrimson and other spur-type apples are considerably hardier in bloom than other types of Delicious apples. In addition the spur-type growth matures earlier in the Fall and has stocky thick twigs so it's not subject to early freezing like many others.

Because it starts bearing the second or third year after planting, Starkrimson will produce twice as much during the first ten years as the present Delicious strains. Apples are of uniform size and true Delicious shape.

Starkrimson is also available in dwarf spur-type trees which are ideal for city lots and home fruit gardens.

Whether you plant the dwarf or the regular Starkrimson type *you'll need to plant another variety of apples close by for pollination purposes.*

Pear trees

Pear trees can be grown espalier style up the side of a wall, just like a grape vine

Bartlett — There is not the slightest doubt that the Bartlett is North America's favourite pear for size and taste. There is hardly a person who doesn't know the Bartlett pear and its qualities. It is grown in, and is adaptable to, many different climates, soils and situations. The fruits of the Bartlett are recognized as being the fanciest and the finest of all pears. Fruits are large, pyramidal in shape and golden yellow in colour with a reddish blush on the sunny side. Flesh is tender, fine grained, buttery, rich and juicy and possesses a delicious musky aroma. Trees are vigorous, grow to a large size, start to bear young and

live for many years. Barring frost during blossom time, they'll bear full crops year after year.

Max Red Bartlett — As mentioned above, everyone knows the Bartlett pear, but now we have a better, special Bartlett pear which features solid bright red colouring. Otherwise, it's almost the same as Bartlett but has a richer, more mellow, true Bartlett flavour. The trees bear young and heavily. It is such a fine pear your friends will exclaim with delight when they see the mahogany red colour of the ripened fruit.

Beurre Bosc — Here is a very popular

Bosc

and produces mature fruit in early September. Extra large, superbly flavoured pears with a scarlet blush, invite you to taste them. Dymond stands straight, is resistant to disease, is self-pollinizing and can be depended upon to produce a bountiful crop of fruit year after year. This is a distinct new variety that is vigorous, hardy and outstanding in every regard.

Collette Pear is one of the most amazing new fruits we have seen. It is everbearing from early Fall to freeze up, and in addition is one of the most delicious pears on the market. Fruits are firm, juicy, and sweet, and do not rot at the core when ripe. Collette pears are ideal for canning and we guarantee you have never tasted a better pear. Fruits are large and smooth textured and will truly surprise your friends and neighbours.

Dymond

Seckel

Clapp's Favorite

pear which has wonderful keeping qualities. A pear which is rated by all as "very good", or by some as "best". It has a long tapering neck and a long stem which allows it to sway in heavy winds without dropping. Colour is a brownish yellow and the flesh is tender, buttery, very juicy, with a rich flavour and pleasing aroma. Bosc has a reputation for being an excellent pollinator and makes an excellent variety for planting with other trees such as the Bartlett and Clapp's Favourite. The trees are slow growers, but they're more productive. You will find the Bosc to be a most delicious eating pear.

Clapp's Favourite — This is a large yellow full-bodied favourite which thrives where other varieties of pears fail. The fruits resemble Bartlett in size and shape and ripen about the middle of August. They hang like golden pendants, inviting you to reach out and bite into the superbly flavoured, fine textured, white, juicy flesh. The trees grow strong and sturdy producing an abundance of delicious fruit every year. This variety of pears is extremely hardy.

Dymond — It has been said that the Dymond is the perfect pear, combining the best qualities of the other varieties. It starts out with large white blossoms in early May,

Plum and Prune trees

Burbank Mammoth Cardinal—a wonderful yellow-fleshed plum

ite plum which is attaining new popularity, especially in the home garden. There is no better plum for making jam or for eating. Its colour is light to dark purplish red with thick bloom. Flesh is yellow in colour, juicy, firm and sweet. Stones are semi-free to free. Fruits ripen around the first of September, are oval in shape and of medium to large size. Trees grow 12 to 15 feet tall, have a round top and are hardy and very productive.

Reine Claude — This is also known as Greengage and is one of the most popular of all plums. The beautiful fruit, large, pale greenish-yellow in colour, will be marked with red if the fruit is thinned and sufficiently exposed to the sun. Trees grow only moderately high, usually about 12 to 15 feet. Plums are usually ripe between the 25th and the 30th of September. They have a luscious eating and canning quality, considered to be the standard of excellence.

Bradshaw is a very large and fine early plum. The fruits have an attractive dark violet skin with contrasting yellow flesh. They are very juicy and excellent for eating and canning. Trees grow vigorously and are very hardy. The Bradshaw plum has the ability to produce heavy crops of delicious

Plums and Prune trees — Plum and prune trees usually start to bear the second or third year after planting, depending on the care they receive and the growth that they make. Distance to plant apart is 20 feet.

With the exception of the prunes of the German and Stanley varieties which are self pollinating, plums need to be interplanted to ensure bearing fruit. Should you decide to plant plum trees, make sure you use European varieties for pollinating that class, and Oriental kinds for those varieties. Burbank and Santa Rosa are typical Oriental varieties. Reine Claude and Lombard are representative European kinds.

Early Golden is a Canadian plum. The plums are free-stone and have good firm flesh. Trees are heavy croppers, and grow very vigorously. This is the first plum to ripen, and the trees are extremely hardy.

Lombard—Here we have an old favour-

Burbank Red Ace Plum

46

Stark Giant Damson Plum makes delicious jams, jellies and preserves

class by itself for eating purposes, and it also has good cooking quality, but unfortunately for this purpose it is not free-stone. Plums will be ready for picking between August 8th and the 15th.

Santa Rosa — No garden is complete without this very promising Oriental variety of plum. Fruits are extremely large, handsome, and dark red in colour with purple overtones. Flesh is very juicy, of good quality and has an attractive red colour. Trees are large, vigorous, and moderately productive. Plums are ripe anytime during the last ten days of August.

Burbank — This is a variety that has been on the market for a considerable time, and yet loses none of its popularity with the passing years. Fruits are very large, especially if thinning is carried out. The best time to thin out is when the plums are small and green, this enhances the colour and quality. Colour is a bright red with some purple overtones. Flesh is meaty and quite firm. Fruits should be picked before they are entirely ripe.

The low growing trees are flat topped, with somewhat drooping branches which make them attractive in the garden from the time they start to flower until the leaves drop in late Fall. There are few varieties of plums which are more productive. Fruits will be ripe during the last week in August.

fruit every year. Ripening time is September 5th to the 10th.

Superior — This plum is exceptionally hardy and is recommended for the Northern and Western States. Fruits are freestone, sweet and juicy. The yellow flesh is covered with wine-red skin. Plant two trees for best results, or if planted singly, is a good pollinizer for other plums. Fruits become ripe early in August.

Prune type Plums

Stanley is an exceptionally productive variety introduced at the New York State Experimental Station. Many garden experts consider it the best prune for home use and commercial planting. Among its better qualities is the fact that it bears fruit in just three years, and ripens ten days earlier than other varieties. The large, deep bluish-

purple fruits are firm and sweet and have a very excellent flavour.

Fellenberg (also known as Italian and German) — This is a widely known and valuable plum for dessert, but most of its reputation is in drying for preserves. Fruits are long, oval, and purple in colour with a thick bloom. Flesh is firm, sweet and pleasant and separates freely from the stone. Trees have moderate growth and crop well. Prunes start to ripen around the 24th to the 27th of September.

Oriental varieties of Plums

Shiro is the golden yellow plum that everyone loves to see and eat. The low-growing hardy trees bear immense crops every year. Fruits have exceptional high quality, are very tender and juicy. The Shiro is in a

Plum trees for much below zero districts—These plums have been developed for VERY COLD DISTRICTS.

Assiniboine — Fruits are bright red, have a yellowish flesh, are quite juicy and of very good quality. They start to ripen about the middle of August. This variety is an excellent pollinizer.

Mount Royal — The trees produce large blue fruits of excellent quality. Flesh is yellow, firm, juicy, sweet and the quality is quite good. Ripening time is the middle of September. This is one of the very hardiest prune plums.

Grenville — Here we have a very high yielding plum whose bright red colour is somewhat like the Oriental variety Burbank. The large tasty fruit measures up to 2 inches in diameter.

Underwood — Trees of Underwood are medium in size and they produce large round fruits whose colour is yellow, overlaid with light to rich red, combined with a faint waxy bloom. Flesh is golden yellow, tender, juicy, sweet and the quality excellent. Fruiting season is the third week in August.

Burbank Grand Prize Prune is large and juicy

Burbank Giant Yellow Plum, early yellow freestone plum

48

Cherry trees

Van Sweet Cherry is super-hardy

Sweet cherries start to bear the third or fourth year after planting. The trees may be planted as close as 25 feet apart. Sweet cherries are not self-pollinating, or the technical name, self unfruitful, and so must be inter-planted with other varieties. Where Napoleon and Emperor Francis are to be planted together, another variety such as Windsor or Black Tartarian must be added, as the first two will not pollinate each other.

Sour cherries begin to bear the second or third year after planting, and should be set 20 feet apart. Sour cherries are self-fruitful, but they will not pollinate sweet cherries, and vice versa.

Black Tartarian is the earliest of all the sweet cherries. This well-known and popular cherry produces very large, bright purplish-black fruits which are juicy and have a rich flavour. Black Tartarian cherries are excellent for canning. Trees are remarkably vigorous and erect growers, and will produce immense crops. Does well on a wide range of soils. Ripening date for Black Tartarian is any time between June 20th and July 4th, depending on your climatic location. One of the big problems with Black Tartarians is the attacks of birds on the cherries. This is mainly because it's the first variety to ripen, and the birds, particularly robins, seem to want to get their fill on the first cherries of the season. Light netting covering the tree and branches seems to be the only satisfactory way of protecting the cherries from the birds.

Emperor Francis is recognized as one of the newer leading sweet cherries for home and commercial orchards. This high quality cherry resembles Napoleon in size and colour, except that its colour is a little darker. You can start to pick the fruit around July 4th.

Napoleon or Royal Ann — Here is a choice sweet cherry which is good for canning and eating. Cherries are large size, pale yellow with a bright red cheek, sweet, juicy and firm. Ripening date is anywhere from July 7th to the 10th.

Windsor — This is one of the best quality dark cherries, and is often referred to as Black Oxheart. It has long been regarded as the main sweet cherry variety. Fruits are large and dark red in colour, almost black, and are sweet, firm and rich. They're delicious to eat fresh and wonderful for canning. The trees grow upright and are rapid and vigorous growers. It's probably as hardy as any sweet cherry, and the ripening date is from July 20th to 26th.

Schmidt's Bigarreau — It would be hard to find a larger variety of sweet cherries. Fruits are produced in clusters and they have a very fine black colour if allowed to remain on the trees until the correct picking time. They are very delicious to eat either fresh or canned, and keep well. Picking time is around the 10th to 12th of July.

Empress Eugenie — Here is a variety of sweet cherry that has been found to be more hardy than any other. It has proven to be hardy even during very cold years when the temperature has dipped as low as 10° below zero. For the home gardener this is a good variety because the tree doesn't ripen all at the one time, but does so gradually, and ripe cherries may be picked over a much longer period of time. Fruits are dark red in colour, tender, meaty, and have a pleasing tart flavour.

Dark, sweet Windsor

49

Sour Cherries — Montmorency —
There is not the slightest doubt in the world
that Montmorency is the best red sour
cherry. These large, dark red, very firm,
fine flavoured cherries are much sought
after by the housewife for pies, canning and
jam purposes. This is the cherry that the
canning factories buy by the hundreds of
tons. Trees are very hardy, standing below
zero temperatures and come into bearing
the second or third year after planting. Sour
cherries as well as sweet cherries need a
well-drained location. If your soil is the
slightest bit on the wet side, don't plant
cherries. On the other hand, if your soil is
stony or gravelly, you can expect much success from cherries. The fruits of Montmorency start to ripen in early to mid-July,
and the blossoms are self fertilizing.

Dwarf Cherry
North Star— This is the cherry to grow
in areas where the climate is very cold.

Schmidt's Bigarreau is a black sweet cherry

North Star is an amazing dwarf tree, growing only 5 to 7 feet high. Cherries are produced by the thousands, having tender flesh
which is juicy and meaty. Colour is bright
red, changing to a deep mahogany red.
Fruit starts to ripen anywhere from July
15th to the first week in August, depending
upon where you live. Excellent for pies and
sauce, the fruits have small stones and hang
well on the tree. This dwarf cherry is a
lovely tree for the garden or border whether
in flower or in fruit. It generally bears the
first year after planting.

Sweet cherries are not self-pollinating

50

Peach trees

These are the fastest growing of all the fruit trees, and they often start to bear the second year after planting. In the home garden they are not only the most useful because of their delicious fruits, but are a real addition to the landscape, especially when covered with glorious pink blossoms in early May. Normal planting distance is 20 feet apart.

Peaches are not reliably hardy where the temperature regularly falls to 10° below zero F., during the Winter. At around 10° below zero the peach buds are killed and below 20° the trees are often killed, especially those not planted in a well drained location. It's a good idea to check with your local nurseryman or government experimental station to see if the climate in your area is suitable for growing peaches.

Red Haven is rapidly becoming the leading, top quality, early peach. It's not only a very early bearer, but also a very productive one. The fruit has a most attractive bright red colour, with an orange background. Peaches are firm, of high quality and have a very delicious taste. Being a free-stone peach, it is also good for canning, as well as eating. You will be picking the fruits any time between August 10th and 15th. Like other peaches, Red Haven usually starts to bear the third year after planting, and you will need to plant at least

The Red Leaf Peach

Stark Early Elberta Peach makes fine eating

51

one other variety with it for cross pollination purposes.

Golden Jubilee — This has been one of the very best peaches ever developed, both for the home garden and for commercial orchards. It's an early yellow, freestone peach of exceptional quality. The fruits have a red blush on the sunny side. There are more Golden Jubilee peach trees now planted than all the other varieties. It's hard to beat either for eating or canning, having fruits which are very long and oblong in shape with a delicious flavour.

Hale-Haven is a marvellous peach resulting from the crossing of the famous J. H. Hale with South Haven. The trees produce large, beautifully coloured yellow-fleshed peaches, which ripen approximately ten days to two weeks ahead of Elberta. Peaches are perfectly free-stone and are of the highest quality. Trees are strong growers and heavy bearers. Peaches start to ripen during the first week in September.

Peach trees are the fastest growing of all fruit trees

Elberta Peaches are a late flowering variety

52

Peach trees are excellent for planting in the garden

Peaches start to bear soon after planting

J. H. Hale is an extra large free-stone peach whose flesh is golden yellow and is delicious in flavour. It must be cross-pollinized with some other variety in order to ensure a crop of peaches. The usual ripening date is between September 17th and 21st.

Fowler — This peach was developed by Mr. George R. Fowler of Marlboro, N.Y. It's a large yellow peach of the Elberta type and is extremely hardy. Trees are vigorous growers, and exceptionally disease resistant. Fruit matures a week later than Elberta and ripens evenly. Peaches are firm, thick skinned and practically fuzzless.

Elberta — This has long been recognized as the best canning peach, is one of the most popular of all peaches, and you will find it planted wherever peaches are grown. Fruits are large, handsome and of high quality. It must be admitted that it is not quite as good an eating peach as Golden Jubilee or Red Haven. Fruits are ready for picking between September 10th and the 20th.

Red Leaf Peach — Here is a special new peach supplying both foliage and fruit of novelty type. The foliage is bright, bronzy red during early Spring and Summer, which gradually changes to maroon in the Fall. The deep rose blossoms contrast delightfully with the colourful foliage. Fruits are also red, with golden markings, are of high quality and good flavour. This sensational tree grows 12 to 15 feet high at maturity, and produces a full crop of perfectly formed, round peaches about 1½ inches across.

Summerlong — This is a sensational new "ever-bearing" peach. Fruits are produced from late July to about September 15th and are medium in size, yellow, free-stone and of excellent quality. The flesh is sweet and tasty, and does not bruise easily. Fruit and blossoms appear on the tree at the same time. The long bearing season allows you to pick fruit for two whole months instead of just a few weeks.

A high quality yellow freestone peach

tree and ripen in mid-August.

Early Golden is a new free-stone apricot which posseses a very fine flavour. Skin is smooth, fuzzless and a pale orange in colour. Fruits are medium to large in size and make very good eating.

Apricot trees

Most home gardeners are not aware that apricots can be grown even in the really cold areas. There are varieties on the market now which will withstand temperatures as much as 30° to 40° below zero, and still produce delicious fruit. Apricots are valuable both for their fruits and as a beautiful ornamental flowering shade tree. It's always necessary to plant two varieties to ensure cross pollination.

Perfection is an outstanding variety with fruits of a rich golden apricot colour, having exceptional size and delicious flavour. The trees start to bear when very young, and are extremely hardy. The original tree at Waterville, Oregon at an elevation of 2,650 feet has withstood temperatures as low as 30° below zero, and extremely rigorous climatic conditions.

Moorpark is a most attractive apricot with high quality and fine flavour. Fruit is large, deep yellow with a red cheek. The trees grow about the same size as a peach

Apricots can be grown even in cold areas

54

Dwarf fruit trees

For the home garden, a dwarf flowering crab apple makes an excellent lawn specimen

can take as long as 10 years before starting to produce apples.

The same pollination problem is common to both dwarf and standard fruit trees. You need at least two different varieties of apples or pears for pollination purposes. Apples will not pollinate pears.

Dwarf fruit trees must always be staked at planting time unless you intend to train them along a fence or a wall in what is called "Espalier" fashion like a grape vine or making the trees grow in a bush form. Staking is done for three reasons, to strengthen the union or graft, to carry the crop of fruit which is generally heavy compared to the size of the trees, and to prevent breakage of the rather brittle roots.

Nurserymen have to do much more work in producing dwarfs than in growing standard trees. The main method is to bud or graft a standard variety of apple or pear to the root of a small-growing variety. In this respect root stock have been investigated more thoroughly for apples than for pears and other fruits.

Delightful Spring blossoms, Summer shade and delicious fruits in the Fall, are the triple values offered by planting fruit trees in the garden. For the beginner to gardening and for the average small garden, the best plan is to plant dwarf fruit trees.

It's true that a dwarf fruit tree will not bear as much fruit as a standard tree, but this can be remedied by planting more trees in the same space, and in the end you will have about the same quantity of fruit. Even our commercial fruit growers have begun to

recognize this fact, and many of them are switching to dwarf or semi-dwarf trees. On the other hand, for the home owner who has the space and wants shade as well as blossoms and fruits, the standard size trees may be preferred.

Certainly dwarf trees will bear very much earlier, usually starting a year after planting. The crop will get larger as the tree grows older. Most standard size trees will take a minimum of 5 years before they bear fruit. Standard size Northern Spy Apples

Pear trees are dwarfed by using quince stock. Some varieties, including the popular Bartlett, do not unite well with quince. In such cases a compatible variety such as Beurre Hardy is first budded on the quince. The desired variety is then budded to Beurre Hardy. Trees about half the size of the standard pear trees are produced.

It's very important when planting the dwarf trees to make sure the bud or graft is 3 to 4 inches above the level of the soil. You can easily locate the point where the graft or the bud was made by finding the bulge on the trunk a few inches above the roots. If you allow the point where the tree was grafted or budded to come in contact with the soil the odds are the tree will no longer be dwarf. Remember that above the bud or graft the tree is just the same as any standard variety and if this part of the tree starts to produce roots then you no longer have a dwarf tree.

For most gardens the fully dwarf trees are the best. Place full-dwarf apples 10 to 12 feet apart each way. Set the semi-dwarf trees 20 feet apart each way.

When planting dwarfs prune them back to keep the top in balance with the roots. A loss of roots always occurs in transplanting. If the trees are single stems 3 to 4 feet high, prune them back to about 30 inches. Generally no further pruning is needed during the first year.

VEGETABLES

VEGETABLES

Tasty fresh vegetables can be grown alongside the flower bed

A good vegetable garden offers many assets to a family. It not only produces fresh, nutritious food but also provides a healthy pastime for those who take part in the growing of the vegetables.

Despite your locality — city, suburbs or country, it is possible to have a vegetable garden which can be a source of pleasure and in the case of some vegetables, a means to making a profit. For instance, you can grow strawberries and sweet corn much cheaper than you can buy them. On the other hand, growing your own potatoes usually does not save money, yet there is no gourmet delicacy in the world to compare to little new potatoes dug fresh from the garden.

Vegetables picked fresh from the garden and cooked immediately contain more vitamins and minerals, are much higher in quality and flavor than those sold on the market.

Vegetable gardening can even be carried out by apartment dwellers who have windows which do not face north. A south window is undoubtedly the best because it will receive the maximum amount of sunshine possible. On the other hand, the west and east windows usually receive sunshine for half the day and will grow a number of vegetables. You need a window box or containers such as flower pots or small seedling flats. In these you can grow mouth-

watering radishes, delectable leaf lettuce, peppercress and other salad ingredients or garnishes. In the pots or seedling flats, vegetables can be grown not only during the Summer, but throughout the year.

The recent developments in fast freezing enable us to enjoy the vegetables at their delicious best, picked fresh from the garden during the growing season, and at the same time we can freeze large quantities for use during the rest of the year. It is most important we take this into consideration when planning the size of the vegetable garden, and the quantity of vegetables to be grown.

Planning the garden

The best time to start planning is just as soon as the seed catalogs arrive in January. This will give you a chance to obtain the seed well ahead of planting time. If you wish to have some plants started indoors by your local plant grower, or have your eye on some special varieties not commonly grown — you will be able to tell your local plant grower of your requirements and he will then have the opportunity to order the seed and have the plants ready for you in the Spring.

It is also a good plan to write to Agricultural Extension Services for any bulletins they may have covering vegetables in the home garden.

There is no doubt that one of the best guides to planning a vegetable garden is a seed catalog from a reliable firm. It will pay

To do a good job of cultivating, hoes should be kept sharp

you to make sure that you are on the mailing list of several companies.

The present trend in good nursery catalogs is to make them as informative as possible and, say you are interested in beets, you would find each variety described in detail. After the name of each particular variety is normally listed the number of days it takes from the time the seed is sown in the garden until roots of ideal eating or bunching size are produced. Also included would be the major cultural directions for the growing of beets in the garden and the amount of seed needed to sow a certain length of row.

In making your plans it is good practice to take a large piece of paper or cardboard and spot in the number of rows and the plants in each row to a rough scale. An important point to keep in mind is to locate the early crops on either the right or the left side of the garden reversing the plan the following year so that you will not grow the same vegetables in the same place two years in succession.

It is also good planning to arrange your vegetable garden so that the rows run north and south. This will give the plants the benefit of as much sun as possible.

Sunshine is an essential factor when growing vegetables. Every part of the garden should receive at least five hours of full sunshine every day. Unfortunately, in many gardens the location of the vegetable garden cannot be changed although parts of it will be shaded by large trees. In such cases, some of the shade can be eliminated by removing the lower limbs of the trees. This

Celery needs a rich, moist soil

The methods of growing cabbage can be applied to broccoli

should provide enough sunlight to allow many types of vegetables to grow successfully.

Size of the garden — It is hard to recommend a definite size because the size of the overall garden varies as much with

Most people have room for a small vegetable plot

the location. In most city gardens there is only room for a very small vegetable garden, whereas in the suburbs or in the country a much larger garden is possible. For small gardens in the city an area 100 square feet would be all there is room for. This could be located in a sunny spot 10 feet by 10 feet, or could even be part of a mixed border 5 feet in width and 20 feet in length. In such a garden it is advisable to grow a succession of quick-growing vegetables that can be closely planted together. These would include radishes, lettuce, green onions, beets, carrots, spinach, bush beans and four or five tomato plants grown on stakes.

Home gardeners living in the country or suburbs and who intend to grow most of

their own vegetables, either to be eaten fresh, canned or fresh frozen, will need a vegetable garden that has an area of 1,500 square feet. This would mean a plot 30 feet long and 50 feet wide or its equivalent.

Good drainage is a must — To be successful in growing vegetables, it is essential that the soil in which they are planted must be well drained. An area where the water lies for a long time in the Spring or after Summer rains should not be used for vegetable gardening. A good indication of poor drainage is the formation of green scum on the surface of the soil or the presence of many cracks after the soil has finally dried out. About the only way a poorly drained area can be changed is to have some tile drain laid which will carry the water away to the nearest outlet.

Getting the soil in shape — There is no doubt that a sandy loam soil containing lots of humus is the best one in which to grow vegetables. Unfortunately, home gardeners usually have to put up with soils which are not nearly as good as sandy loam. This does

not mean that these soils cannot be conditioned to grow vegetables. Both the light sandy soils and the heavy clay ones are improved in the same way, by digging in large quantities of humus.

Just as soon as the soil can be worked in the Spring is the time to dig in the humus. In the lighter soils which tend to dry out quickly, the addition of humus acts like a sponge in the soil, helping to retain the moisture and at the same time preventing the plant food dissolved in it from being leached away too quickly.

In the heavy soils the humus opens them up, improves the drainage and permits the vital oxygen to circulate more freely through the soil and readily reach the roots of the plants.

For humus any one of the following will prove satisfactory: material processed from sewage, peat moss, well-rotted barnyard manure, discarded mushroom manure, or compost. For those gardens which are fortunate enough to have reasonable top soil, the humus should be applied at the rate of 6 to 8 bushels per hundred square feet. In gardens where the earth is almost sub-soil

Brilliant red peppers make a spectacular show in the garden

Good drainage is a must for growing vegetables

of August and then a Fall crop of rye grass sown. Although the rye will be several inches high by the time the growing season ends in late Fall, it will live over the Winter and can be turned under the next May when it grows to about two feet high.

This plan can be worked in any garden after early crops of vegetables such as peas have been harvested. The soil is prepared as suggested above, the rye grass seed sown and before long a nice crop of bright green rye grass plants are coming along.

Any of these methods can be easily carried out by the newest beginner to gardening and will do a great deal towards improving the soil conditions found in the garden.

Planting & care of vegetables

The time to plant your early vegetables will depend on their hardiness and the temperatures in your own area. Since Spring can be early one season and late another, it is hard to recommend an exact planting time. Spring can also come much earlier depending on the climate where you live. The average date of the last killing frost and soil temperature is the best method of determining the right planting date.

Regardless of the late frosts, any of the following hardy vegetables can be planted just as soon as the soil can be prepared:

    Asparagus roots
    Cabbage seeds and plants
    Kale seeds and plants

Seed can either be broadcast or sprinkled in shallow furrows

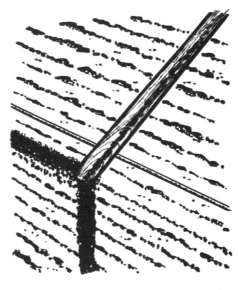

10 bushels per 100 square feet will not be too much.

Your vegetable garden will not only need quantities of humus in the soil, but should be well supplied with plant food. Best way of ensuring this is to dig in with the humus a fairly large amount of complete fertilizer at the rate of 4 pounds per 100 square feet.

For a small garden, say 10 feet by 10 feet in area, the best idea is to spade the humus and fertilizer into the soil. For larger gardens, the ideal way is to use rotary tilling equipment. These machines will thoroughly mix the soil, the fertilizer and the humus together and leave it in a "ready-to-plant" condition. However, the use of such equipment puffs up the soil considerably and you will need to rake the soil two or three times to take out the puffiness and to level it.

Other ways of improving the soil —

For people who have moved into a new home and wish to condition their soil inexpensively, there is another way of improving the soil, particularly where the soils are either very light or very heavy.

Just as soon as the soil can be worked, apply humus as mentioned before at the rate of six bushels per 100 square feet and a complete fertilizer at the rate of 4 pounds per 100 square feet. Mix the top eight inches of the soil, the fertilizer and humus thoroughly together. Rake level, and then thickly sow a crop of rye grass which is obtainable from any seedsman, or country feed dealer. The rye will quickly germinate and when it gets 18 to 24 inches high, it can be ploughed under to build up the supply of humus in the soil.

For people who buy a house some time after the end of June the soil can be worked up in a similar manner around the middle

A rope or wire line will help you keep rows straight

For large seeds the hoe can be used to fill in the furrows

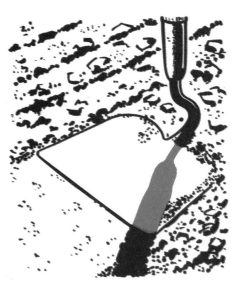

The back of the hoe will do a good job of firming the soil around the seeds

Onion sets and seed
Spinach
Turnips
Rhubarb roots
Horseradish roots

In most seasons garden peas and sweet peas can be planted just as soon as the soil is workable and you will have success. The only disappointment you might have in planting peas early is the odd year when there is a lot of rain right after planting, and this would cause the seed to rot.

Next to be planted are a group of what we call "half-hardy" vegetables. These are the kind that will stand a light frost—but not a really heavy one. A safe date for planting these is a week to 10 days before the average date of the last killing frost. This group would include:

Beets
Carrot seed
Cauliflower plants
Celery plants
Swiss Chard seed
Parsnip seed
Second sowing of peas
Radish seed
Early potatoes
Lettuce plants

Snap beans and sweet corn are tender vegetables which should be planted only *after* the date of the last killing frost. Unless the weather is warm, neither one of these vegetables will grow very fast so there is really no point in trying to rush the season.

The final group is classed as very tender and in all but the warmer areas should not be planted until after the 24th of May.

Cucumber
Eggplant
Lima beans
Muskmelon
Pepper plants

Pumpkins
Squash
Tomato plants
Watermelon

For the really keen gardener, taking soil temperatures with a soil thermometer can

Tomatoes are usually planted after the 24th of May

62

The red pepper Vinedale

Most seeds are covered with soil to a depth of three times their diameter

Be sure and mark each vegetable after sowing

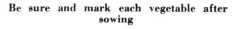

also serve as a planting guide. The following minimum temperatures are required for germination:

32°—Lettuce, onion, parsnip and
    spinach.
40°—Beets, cabbage, carrots, parsley,
    radish, Swiss chard and turnip.
50°—Sweet corn, and tomato seed.
60°—Lima beans, snap beans, cucum-
    bers, muskmelon, squash and
    watermelon.

You can plant the seed of a given vegetable when soil temperatures have risen to the minimum for germination. However, we would say your chances for a successful early vegetable crop will be best if you combine the above-mentioned guides covering the last killing frost date and soil temperatures.

A pure white head of fresh cauliflower

Transplanted vegetables

Celery will improve any salad

There are many vegetables which need to be started indoors from seed like annuals and then transplanted outdoors in order to produce early yields. As a matter of fact, there are quite a number that will not produce a satisfactory yield in the colder areas unless they are handled this way. These are:

Tomatoes
Peppers
Broccoli
Cabbage
Cauliflower
Head lettuce
Celery
Eggplant
Onions

Especially in the cooler parts of the country, it is also a good plan to handle cucumber, muskmelon or watermelon plants in this way.

For the beginner to home gardening, it is better to buy well-grown plants rather than attempting to grow his own plants from seed sown indoors. Your local horticultural society or garden club will be able to give you the names of reliable nurseries, garden centers, seed stores or plant growers from whom good plants can be purchased.

How do you recognize good plants? —Buy short, stocky plants that are a healthy green in color and by all means avoid those that are tall and spindly. They should have good root systems and have been hardened off. Hardened plants are created by gradually subjecting them to cooler temperatures over a two or three week period. Such plants will be able to survive any sudden drop in temperature close to the freezing mark, or even two or three degrees below.

When transplanting the vegetables from the container to the garden, it is most impor-

When harvesting peppers, always use pruning shears or a sharp knife

to gardening firm the soil quite heavily at this point and they literally "hang" the plants.

By firming the soil around the roots we eliminate any air pockets that might exist which can either prevent the plants from getting off to a quick start or even kill them.

What are starter solutions? These are concentrated, complete all soluble fertilizers that have a high phosphorus content which help the plants get off to a quick start, and in the end produce larger and earlier yields. Such solutions are available as liquid fertilizers or you can make your own by mixing a half cup of a complete dry fertilizer in six quarts of water.

Beating the season — There is a way of beating the season for tomatoes, peppers, eggplants, muskmelons and watermelons. Plants of these vegetables can be set out in the garden two or three weeks ahead of the normal planting date and covered with polyethylene tents or hotcaps which will help to warm up the soil quickly and protect the vegetables from light frosts and cold winds. Just as soon as the danger of frost is

tant to keep as much soil as possible around the roots. The best results are achieved if you do not disturb the plants any more than necessary. Plants started in clay pots, peat pots or veneer plant bands can be moved to the garden with almost no injury and will never really know that they have been moved. On the other hand, plants grown in seedling flats or plant boxes holding about a dozen vegetables usually receive at least a week's setback before they recover.

Cucumbers or melons are best started in veneer plant bands which have four sides but no top or bottom. The bands are quite fragile and can be easily removed with the soil remaining practically intact and the root system undisturbed.

In transplanting, always set the vegetables slightly deeper than they grew in the container or seedling flat. Cover the roots with a little soil and pour about a cup of "starter solution" into the hole around each plant before filling in the remainder of the soil. Then pack the earth firmly around the plant. This firming should be done around the edges of the earth or root ball rather than at the point where the stem and surface of the soil come together. Most newcomers

past, the protection should be removed for a few hours each day to gradually harden the plants. Then when the weather turns warm, the protection should be removed altogether.

Spacing your vegetables — Most vegetables such as carrots and beets which are grown from seed are not only sown too thick in the beginning, but are usually left the same way after they have germinated and come through the ground. When a large number of plants compete with each other for moisture, food and growing space, they could be considered weeds and would do almost as much damage. It is hard for many

Other common vegetables should be spaced as follows:

Snap beans—3 inches between plants

Bush lima beans—8 inches between plants

Kale—4 inches between plants

Lettuce—3 inches between plants

Spinach—3 inches between plants

To sum up, in thinning vegetables, we have to remember that a plant must have sufficient room to spread out its leaves to get the maximum effects of sunshine, and there should be enough room for the roots so there will not be too much competition from other plants for the moisture and available plant food.

Cultivation

Frequent cultivation is essential when growing vegetables. Weeds must be destroyed as soon as they appear through the soil so they will not rob the vegetable plants of precious plant food and moisture. Cultivation just as soon as the soil surface has dried after rain, or watering from the hose, will prevent the soil from forming a hard crust and give the air a chance to circulate much needed oxygen through the particles of earth and so reach the roots. In most areas the first weeds start to show up around the 20th to the 24th of May.

When cultivating, be sure to do it shal-

Growing instructions for squash also apply to vegetable marrow

people to be ruthless when the plants are small and so do not thin them correctly.

However, carrots should be thinned to two inches apart and beets to three inches apart. The best time to do this is when the plants first come through the ground. You will discover those you leave will not only grow much faster, but will be more tender and have a better flavor.

Correct thinning of other vegetables is also important. Early sweet corn should be spaced so that there is one stalk for each 10 inches of row. With the later varieties, you should allow not more than one stalk for each 14 inches of row.

Beets should be thinned to 3″ apart

lowly at all times, particularly after the middle of June when the vegetable plants have developed feeding roots close to the surface of the soil.

Chemicals are not recommended for weed control in the home garden. These selective weed killers are practical only where there are large fields of one vegetable. A chemical that is safe for one kind of vegetable can severely injure or kill another kind close by, or even in a row alongside the treated ones.

The best hand tool for cultivating is a Dutch hoe which consists of a sharp blade held in the form of a "D" at the end of a long handle. Such a hoe enables the home gardener to cultivate backwards, thus eliminating any shoe marks. He will also be able to cultivate as shallowly as needed.

Mulching

Covering the surface of the soil between the vegetable rows and plants with fibrous or plastic mulches will assist in cutting out some cultivation and also help to preserve the amount of moisture in the soil. It is best for the home gardener to cultivate freely up until about the 20th of June and then apply a mulch 3 or 4 inches deep.

Watering

To grow top quality vegetables which not only yield well but have a good flavor, the soil must contain at all times a uniform supply of moisture. When adequate rain does not fall, the home gardener must be prepared to water the garden at least once a week. Avoid daily light sprinklings which merely encourage surface rooting and provide little or no benefits for the plants.

The amount of water applied will depend on the depth required. For instance, early in the season the roots will be close to the surface and the moisture will only have to

sprinkled on the soil too fast it will form a more or less impervious cover which will prevent any further moisture from entering the ground. The excess water just runs off to the nearest drain and is wasted.

Feeding

In addition to adding a quantity of complete fertilizer to the soil before seeding or planting vegetables you will have to make further feedings once a month during the growing season. The number of times you feed will depend on how long it takes the particular vegetable to reach maturity. Best

Cauliflowers need lots of humus and fertilizer in the soil

Early maturing vegetables such as lettuce, radishes, spinach, early cabbage and potatoes do not benefit from mulching because they are harvested in June or early July before the mulch has had sufficient time to be effective. The greatest advantages received from mulching are that it reduces the need for constant cultivation, preserves moisture in the soil, and protects the roots from the hot July and early August sun.

penetrate the soil to a depth of four or five inches. This is the situation which prevails during the month of June. In July, the moisture would have to sink to a depth of six or seven inches. In early August, eight to ten inches would be the right depth.

One of the best ways of applying the water is to lay a plastic or canvas soaker between the rows and let it gradually release the water at a rate which it can be absorbed by the soil. It is a mistake to stand with the hose and try to water the vegetable garden. It is not generally realized that if water is

way to make such feedings is to scatter a complete fertilizer two inches on either side of each row. For these row applications use 2 to 3 pounds of complete fertilizer per 50 feet of row. Then take a Dutch hoe and gently work the fertilizer into the surface of the soil. Where mulches have been put in place the fertilizer could be scattered on top of the mulch and then watered in. Where plastic mulches have been used, the material can be lifted up and the fertilizer scattered along the surface of the soil and worked in with a Dutch hoe before replacing the mulch material.

A late vegetable garden

Not all vegetables have to be Spring planted. In early July a Fall garden can be started. The following vegetables can be used for such a purpose:

Kale
Beets
Turnips
Leaf lettuce
Chinese cabbage
Swiss chard
Endive
Snap beans

No special care is required. You prepare the soil exactly the same way as you would in the Spring and give the various vegetables the same treatment as mentioned before.

THE HOME VEGETABLE GARDEN

Garden peas

There is no doubt garden peas are among the most tasty and popular of all garden vegetables. They belong to the legume family which also include beans, alfalfa, soy beans, clover and many other cultivated and wild crops.

This most delicious of garden vegetables originated in the cooler parts of eastern Europe and Western Asia. Its history can be traced back for many thousands of years. For instance, it was a most popular crop during the Stone Age and cave man days. North American Indians were already growing peas when Jacques Cartier made his famous voyage of discovery up the St. Lawrence River in 1534.

The earlier garden peas are set in the ground the better they will grow and produce. This is a vegetable which likes the cool weather of early Spring and should be planted just as soon as it is possible to work the soil. Do not worry about the late Spring frosts, because garden peas can take a light frost without harm. As a matter of fact, they will stand a light frost much more readily than an early heat wave occurring towards the end of May or in early June.

The home gardener should take a tip from the commercial grower and inoculate the seed with nitrogen-fixing bacteria which will increase both the growth of the plants and the yield.

Innoculating the pea seeds is simple and easy. Seedsmen and garden centers everywhere carry inexpensive innoculants with full instructions. The job only takes 15 minutes at the most. Once you have tried innoculating the pea seed you are certain to make it part of the yearly garden work.

There are two ways of extending the picking season for garden peas. You can make three or four sowings a week to ten days apart, or you can plant varieties that take different lengths of time to mature.

Garden peas are heavy feeders and this means you will have to dig in plenty of humus and complete fertilizer ahead of time as mentioned in a previous chapter.

After mixing the soil, humus and complete fertilizer thoroughly together give the soil a final levelling with the garden rake and it will be ready to sow. Plant the seeds 2 inches deep and 3 inches apart in the row.

Support — Dwarf varieties like Little Marvel do not require any support, but the taller growing kinds such as Telephone will have to be supported. To avoid damage to the plants later on, and actually stimulate growth, the support should be set in place at the same time the seed is sown. For this purpose you can use any kind of twiggy brush which will give the peas lots of little twigs on which to cling and climb. Poultry netting or a similar fencing material is also excellent for this purpose. It has an advantage in that it can be rolled up at the end of the pea season and put away for another year.

Make sure that the bottom of such netting reaches to within two or three inches from the soil.

You need plenty of humus to grow garden peas like this

68

Progress is a hardy large-podded variety

are produced. These are borne mostly double, are 3 inches long and ⅝ of an inch wide. These plump, straight pods contain 6 to 8 sweet, juicy and deliciously flavored peas. Little Marvel also freezes well.

Thomas Laxton—An extra high quality all purpose variety which is the best pea for freezing. It is always a heavy cropper and in some seasons it outyields many of the large podded varieties. The vines grow 3 to 3½ inches long, straight, well-filled and dark green in color. Each pod contains 7 to 9 tender peas of the finest flavor. There is no better variety for the home garden, market garden, shipping, canning or freezing.

Laxton's Progress — Hundredfold. A special strain of Laxton's Progress which you may find listed under other names in some seed catalogs. However, if you remember to ask for "special strain", you will receive this variety. It is the earliest and by far the best of the large-podded, large fruited, wrinkled peas. Pods grow 4½ inches long on attractive dark green vines which grow 18 inches high. This improved

Alaska — This is the variety which gives the earliest and hardiest peas and is the surest to make a fair yield. It is also resistant to fusarium wilt. Fifty-five days after sowing the seed you will be picking the well rounded pods. These are produced singly, are a light green in color and straight. They contain 6 to 8 round smooth, bluish-green peas. Vines are a light yellowish-green and grow about 30 inches high. Unfortunately they are not so sweet as the wrinkled seeded varieties nor is the quality as high. Best plan is to make your first sowing of peas Alaska and then switch to varieties of better quality. This will provide several tasty meals of early peas a week to ten days ahead of any other variety.

Little Marvel — This has been a fine variety for over 60 years and it still the most satisfactory pea for the average home garden. Its big advantage is its ability to remain in prime picking condition a week longer than most other kinds. It takes 60 days from the time the seed is sown until the pods are ready for picking.

Little Marvel is a dwarf variety having vines which grow 16 to 18 inches tall and do not need staking. The foliage is dark green and quantities of dark green well filled pods

Garden peas are among the most popular vegetables

strain has disease resistance and is very high yielding. It takes 62 days from the time the seed is sown until the peas are ready for eating.

Tall Telephone (or Alderman) — An ideal high quality green pea of unsurpassed flavor which holds its green color well during cooking. It is the tallest growing variety of peas and is considered the best for staking. Vines grow from 40 to 60 inches in height, are robust, dark green and wilt resistant. Pods grow 4 to 5 inches and more in length, are straight, pointed and well filled with 8 to 10 extra large, sweet tasting peas. This variety does best in the cooler parts of the country, as do all of the tall growing varieties.

Wando — This variety is the most productive hot weather pea. It grows 24 inches in height and will produce a large crop of well-filled pods about 3 inches long when other varieties have dried out owing to hot weather. Pods are dark green, blunt, well filled and contain seven or eight tender medium sized peas of fine quality. They are excellent for fresh use, canning and freezing. Takes 68 days to mature.

Progress No. 9 — This is sometimes called Greater Progress. It is an improved wilt resistant strain of Laxton's Progress which is earlier, hardier and slightly taller than the standard large-podded variety. Pods grow 4½ inches long and are filled with 7 to 9 peas of a most delicious flavor. The vines grow 20 inches tall, and bear peas ready for picking 60 days after the seed is sown.

Lincoln (or Homesteader) — This is a vigorous mid-season, large crop variety. Pods are ready for picking 65 days after the seed is sown and they normally contain 8 to 9 exceptionally fine flavored peas. These are most suitable for the home garden and for freezing. Lincoln can be started earlier, and stand the hot weather better than most other varieties. Vines grow from 24 to 30 inches in height.

Edible podded or sugar peas — The pods of this type of pea are cooked and eaten like snap beans. They possess the tenderness and fleshy podded qualities of a snap bean yet have flavor and sweetness of fresh green peas. When young, the pods are stringless, brittle, succulent and free of fiber

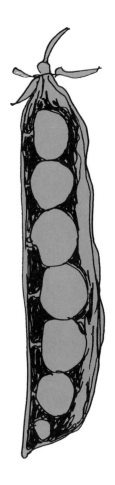

and parchment. At this stage, the peas are not shelled but cooked and eaten in the pods. Should the pods develop too fast for cooking the seeds, which reach their best flavor before they become full size, may be eaten as shell peas.

Giant or Mammoth Sugar—A prolific variety for the home garden. Pods are ready for use 75 days from the time the seed is sown. The vines grow 3 to 4 feet in height, and bear an abundance of large size, sweet and tender pods. These are often sliced before cooking, just like snap beans.

Dwarf Sugar is the earliest and most dwarf growing sugar pea. Pods range from 2½ to 3 inches in length, are light green in color, curved, sweet and tender. Vines grow 2 to 2½ feet tall and are very heavy producers. This is an ideal variety for home gardens, especially where space is limited and seasons are short.

To avoid damage later on, set in supports at the time of planting

70

Tomatoes

In almost any garden, large or small there is room to grow a few tomato plants. No tomatoes you buy ever compare in flavor and quality with the fresh, red ripe ones you pick from your own vines.

People with very small gardens often say they do not have room to grow tomatoes. This is probably true if the plants are allowed to sprawl over the ground, thus taking up considerable space. However, in most gardens, no matter how small, there is room for five or six plants staked and located at the back or end of the annual or mixed border. You will find that these plants will not look out of place and will supply the average family of 5 with all the tomatoes they can use.

In all but the cooler parts of North America, where the season is short hybrid varieties are the best tomatoes to grow. They are strong vigorous growers that have proven ability to outyield the regular varieties but make no mistake about it, the extra yields come largely from the soil. The hybrids produce larger plants and higher yields and this means that they are going to need more feeding than the standard kinds.

Tomatoes are warm weather plants, so there is no particular advantage to be

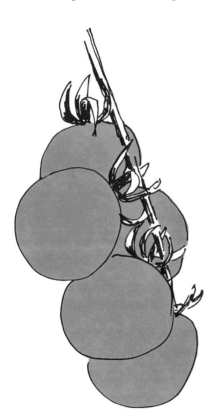

gained in setting them out in the garden before the soil has warmed up. In many areas this would be around the 24th of May, but in any case they should not be planted until the frost-free days and nights have arrived.

Tomatoes came originally from Brazil where the climate is hot, and so the soil must be really warm before the plants will start to grow actively. Very often, if planted too soon, the plants will literally turn blue because of the cold soil and air temperatures, following this experience they will take two or even three weeks to recover.

Tomatoes must be planted in soil which contains plenty of humus and fertilizer. Before planting, work into the soil a large quantity of humus and a complete fertilizer. This should be thoroughly mixed into the top 7 or 8 inches of the soil. A week or ten days after the tomatoes are planted they should receive a further feeding with a complete fertilizer. Scatter a small handful around each plant and gently work it into the soil. Three or four weeks later, make a second application as above.

What kind of plants should I buy?
— This will depend to a large extent on whether you want early or late tomatoes. For early tomatoes, the best method is to buy short stocky plants which have been grown in 3 to 4 inches plant bands, peat pots, or clay pots. These should have been hardened off and just showing their first buds.

Do not buy plants whose first set of flowers are in full bloom because these often fail to set fruit owing to the shock of transplanting.

Unless you have an electric hot bed, or small greenhouse facilities it is better to buy early plants rather than attempt to grow your own.

Tomatoes are warm weather plants

For late tomatoes, the home gardener can sow seed and get good results. The easiest and best way is to obtain some of the new peat pots and fill these with a suitable soil mixture. The commercial African Violet soil mixture would be right for this purpose. The peat pots should be filled to within $\frac{1}{2}$ inch of the top and the soil firmed gently down. Then make a small hole with your finger in the center about $\frac{1}{8}$ of an inch deep. Drop two seeds in each hole and cover with soil. Give the peat pots a thorough soaking with water at room temperature and place in a warm spot to await germination.

When in the majority of cases, both seeds germinate you should leave the stronger and healthier one, removing the weaker. Just as soon as germination takes place the plants should be given a location in full sunshine and a temperature around 70°.

Once the **outdoor** temperatures rise to 65°, the plants can be moved during the warm parts of the day to a sunny spot in the garden, and taken back indoors at night.

Stake tomatoes are pruned to one stem and the stake should be put in place at the time of planting

Tomatoes and other vegetables are best grown in peat pots or other containers

After the 24th of May and the danger of night frost is past, they can be left outside continuously.

About the middle of June, the plants will be ready for setting in the garden. They will start to produce red ripe tomatoes during the latter part of August.

Should tomato plants be staked or allowed to sprawl naturally over the ground? For most small gardens, it is better to stake them. Such plants will produce fruit a week to 10 days sooner and will not take nearly as much room. Tomato plants that are to be

A well drained garden soil, rich in humus will grow good tomatoes

Top conditioning of the soil produces extra yields of tomatoes

tially shade the plants.

After the plants have started active growth in late June it is advisable to mulch them. Before applying the mulch, give them a final shallow cultivation to get rid of any weeds. Tomato roots grow near the surface of the soil and deep cultivation can injure them seriously. Any of the materials used for adding humus to the soil will make a good mulch. To be effective, it should be at least 3 inches deep. Such a mulch will end the need for cultivating, keep the roots cooler and help preserve the moisture in the soil.

There is a new hormone spray on the market which stops blossom drop and makes the flowers set many more fruits. It also makes the tomatoes ripen earlier, become larger and firmer, with many of them being seedless. This hormone is available in an aerosol can, so all you have to do is pick up the can, push the button and spray the blossoms as they open.

Late tomatoes go on producing fruits right up until frost, and very often at this time there will be a good supply of green tomatoes on the vine which you hesitate to waste. You can extend the tomato season until almost Christmas by picking these and storing them in a cool moist and dark place. Notice we said "in a dark place"—because many people have the mistaken idea that tomatoes ripen quicker in a sunny window, and this is a fallacy.

Pick the tomatoes with the stems attached

staked can be set much closer together. The recommended distance apart in the row is from 18 inches to 24 inches depending on the vigor of the variety. Space the rows 2 feet apart.

Staked tomatoes should be pruned to one stem, and the stake put in place at the time of planting. If you wait until the plant has grown and then attempt to put the stake in place, you can cause serious damage to the rather shallow root system. Stakes should be long enough so that they extend 6 feet above the ground. Place the stake close to and on the west side of the plant.

As the plants grow, a loose loop of string, or some other tie material should be made under each fruit cluster and around the stake. Whatever you do, do not make

this too tight or the main stem of the plant can be girdled, and the plant will either die or become stunted.

Once the plants begin to grow rapidly, you will notice that sucker, or what is often called axil growth, will start to form between the main stem and the leaves. This should be removed just as soon as it appears.

In large gardens where it is not necessary to stake tomatoes, the plants should be set 3 feet apart each way and allowed to sprawl over the ground. During some years the hot sun causes the blossoms to fall and not set fruit. To offset this it is a good plan to set the plants to the east of north and south rows of sweet corn, or on the north side of east and west rows so that the corn can par-

Just as soon as the young suckers form on stake tomatoes, they should be removed

and store in a hamper or field crate. To color the tomatoes, take them into a warm well lighted room for a few days, but do not put them in a sunny window.

About the only disease problem you can have with tomatoes is an attack of leaf blight. This is the same fungus disease which attacks potatoes. It only becomes a problem in seasons when there is heavy rainfall. The best way of keeping the blight under control during damp weather is to spray or dust the plants every 5 or 6 days with an all-purpose fungicide.

Burpee's Big Boy — The largest of the hybrid tomatoes, with many of the fruits weighing one pound, and the odd one weighing as much as two pounds. Unlike other large-fruited varieties, Big Boy tomatoes are perfectly smooth, have a deep globe shape and are very firm. Its color is scarlet red and the thick skins enclose bright red meaty flesh of fine flavor and excellent quality.

Big Boy will be at its peak of fruiting in mid-season, and it will continue to produce large fruits late in the season when many of the standard varieties decline in yield and size.

A slice of fresh home grown tomato enhances any meal

Some tomatoes weigh one pound or more

74

Plants are very large, extremely vigorous, semi-upright to spreading with enough foliage to protect the fruits from sun scald.

Pink Beefsteak (or Ponderosa) — People who are unable to eat many kinds of tomatoes because they have a high acid content should grow for themselves one of the beefsteak varieties. Pink Beefsteak or Ponderosa as it is called in some catalogs, has a delicious non-acid and mild flavor. This is a late maturing tomato which takes 80 days from the time the seed is sown until the first fruits are ripe. Because of its lateness, it is not recommended for growing in the colder parts of the country where the growing season is short.

It is not unusual for the purplish-pink fruits of Ponderosa to weight 24 ounces and more, the average will be just over half a pound. The seed cavities are remarkably small which accounts for the solid luscious flesh of a delightful mild flavor. Although the fruits are large in size, they are a very fine quality, tasty and palatable.

Bush Beefsteak — This is the variety to grow where the season is short. It takes

To extend tomato season, pick them when green and store in a cool, dark, moist place

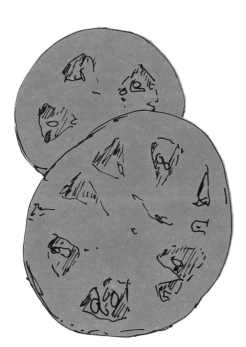

One of the most dangerous diseases for tomatoes is late blight

just 62 days from seeding until the fruits are ready for picking. Bush Beefsteak produces strong, vigorous, compact, bushy plants which hold their extra large meaty fruits well off the ground. The vines while very dwarf and restricted are strong and sturdy. The fruits weigh from one half to over one pound. The rich red solid interior contains very few seeds. This is not only a good variety to grow in areas where the season is short, but it is also of real value in home gardens where there is not too much space.

Burpee's Big Early — Here is a new early hybrid which produces fruits of main crop size just 62 days after seeding. Big Early tomatoes average just under 8 ounces for the entire season, with some fruits weighing up to one pound. They are globular in shape, very smooth and ripen to a bright scarlet right up to the stem. The walls are thick, bright and cover a deep

red interior which is meaty and has an excellent flavor. This variety is an outstanding, firm slicer. Plants are large, vigorous with dark green foliage.

Stokesdale — A new strain which has been specially selected for earliness, large size and heavy yields. The flesh is a rich red color and the vines are vigorous and highly productive. Fruits are smooth, solid, deep round and highly colored. This is an excellent variety for the home gardener to grow.

Sanmarzano — The Sanmarzano tomato is an excellent kind to use for making distinctive salads. Fruits are rectangular in shape, measuring about $3\frac{1}{2}$ inches long and $1\frac{1}{2}$ inches across. They are non-cracking, flat sided and borne in clusters. You would have to say that these were the most intense red of all the commercial tomatoes. Grow them in your garden and

you will discover that they are exceptionally meaty, free from juicy pulp, and very mild in flavor. The ripe fruits are long lasting, both on the vine and in storage. Sanmarzano takes 80 days from the time the seed is sown until you start picking the fruit.

Red Cherry — Gets its name from the shape and size of the fruits which closely resemble a sour red cherry. They are wonderful for salads, preserving, pickling or chilling and eating whole. Fruits are round, scarlet in color and about $\frac{7}{8}$ of an inch in diameter. Seventy-two days after the seed is sown, the first fruits are ripe.

Yellow Pear—Starts to bear fruit about 70 days after seeding. The tomatoes have an exceedingly mild and pleasing flavor which is sweet and delicious. They are yellow, pear-shaped with a definite neck. The fruits average $1\frac{3}{4}$ of an inch to 2 inches in length and about 1 inch in diameter.

Yellow Plum — Bushes of the Yellow Plum variety are extremely productive and the fruits are small, fleshy, approximating the size and shape of a plum. They usually grow 2 inches long, $1\frac{1}{2}$ inches across and have a bright lemon-yellow skin. Their sweet and delicous flavor makes them excellent for use in salads, for chilling and eating whole.

Burpee's Jubilee — A variety high in vitamins whose fruits are a bright golden orange in color. If you have not enjoyed the delicious flavor and good eating qualities of the orange-colored tomato be sure to grow it. In shape, smoothness quality, firmness and heavy yields, Jubilee compares favorably with the best of the standard red varieties. Fruits are deep, globular in shape, 2 inches to $3\frac{1}{4}$ inches in diameter, $2\frac{1}{2}$ inches to $2\frac{3}{4}$ inches in depth and heavy. The orange-colored interior is very high in vitamins A and C.

Burpee's Sunray—One of the few other orange-colored large size tomatoes. It is the same size and color as Burpee's Jubilee mentioned above. It also has the same fine qualities to which wilt resistance has been added. The fruits are globular in shape and grow $2\frac{1}{2}$ inches to $3\frac{1}{4}$ inches in diameter.

Red cherry and Yellow Pear tomatoes add variety and color to a salad

Snap beans

Snap beans are easy to grow and germinate quickly

the home garden you can make the rows as close together as 18 inches. Cover the seeds with fine soil and firm it over them either with your foot or the back of a hoe or rake. Just as soon as the bean plants reach 2 to 3 inches in height thin them to 5 inches apart. An average packet of seed will sow about 25 feet of row: 1 pound to 150 feet.

The latest fertilizer placement tests reveal that the very best results are obtained when a complete fertilizer is placed in furrows 2 inches to each side of the seed row. This fertilizer furrow should be deep enough to allow the placing of the plant food 1½ inches below that of the planted seed.

Under this row feeding method the seed is planted first and covered while the string or wire marker is in place. Then the fertilizer furrows are made and the plant food distributed in them and covered. Apply it at the rate of 1 lb. (approximately 1 pint) per 50 foot row.

One of the most successful vegetable crops for any home gardener to grow are the snap beans, which are also called stringless bush beans. At one time they used to be known as string beans, but now that the tough fiber and strings have been taken out of these varieties by our plant breeders, they are universally called snap beans.

Why the name "snap"? Take a pod green or yellow, break it between your fingers and see how it snaps.

Where a continuous supply of tender beans is required, planting should be made at ten day intervals from May 15th to August 1st. In the short season areas you will not be able to plant as soon, or as late.

The seed requires a minimum temperature of 60° for germination in one week. They will not germinate satisfactorily if planted too deeply, or if the ground is too cold or wet, so there is no point in trying to plant early to beat the season.

Seed should be planted one inch deep and spaced 3 inches apart in the row. In

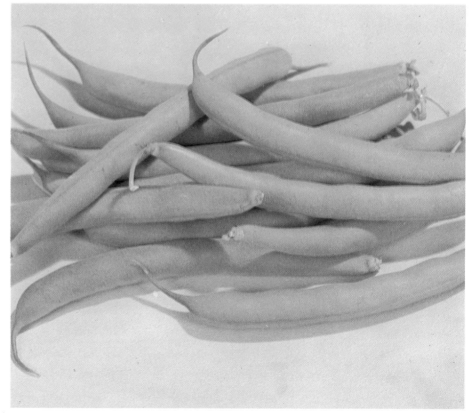

Tender Pod is one of the best flavored snap beans

Green varieties

Tender Crop is one of the newest and best of the green varieties of snap beans. The attractive green pods measure $5\frac{1}{2}$ inches long. They are nearly straight, round, dark green and smooth. Pods are brittle, stringless and have an unusually fine flavor. Tests have shown that Tender Crop is an excellent variety for canning and freezing. The disease resistant plants give a high yield of beans which remain in good edible condition for a long time. Forty-six days after the seed is set in the ground, the beans will be ready for picking.

Tender Pod — This is one of the best flavored of all green snap beans. It takes 50 days from the time the seed is sown until picking commences.

The pods of this variety are brittle, fleshy, stringless, fibreless and $4\frac{1}{2}$ inches to $5\frac{1}{2}$ inches long. They are thick and round, smooth, deep green in color and have unusually long curving tip ends. This is a variety which seems less affected by adverse weather conditions than any other.

Contender—One of the earliest of the green beans. It only takes 41 days after the seed is sown until the beans are ready for eating. The attractive smooth, oval green pods are $5\frac{1}{2}$ inches to 7 inches in length. They are resistant to common bean "mosaic" and powdery mildew.

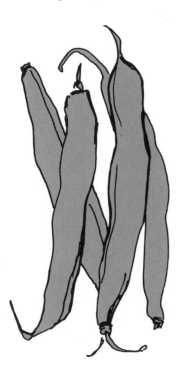

Pencil Pod Wax is a vigorous grower

Every home garden should have green and yellow snap beans

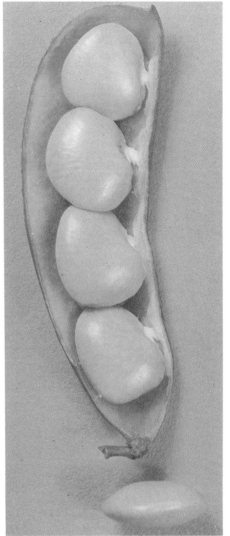

Lima beans freeze well

Yellow varieties

These yellow pod snap beans were formally known as wax beans or butter beans and they are still very popular. Every garden should not only have some green snap beans, but some of the yellow kinds as well. They will give you extra flavor as well as a nice change of color.

Cherokee Wax— This is considered the heaviest producer of the yellow wax varieties. The pods are 6½ inches long, oval in shape, straight, very tender and the quality is excellent. Plants are vigorous and heavy producers.

Choctaw — This has a remarkable ability to give extremely high yields under hot weather conditions. This variety is quite similar to Cherokee, with the exception that it is slightly earlier and the pods are more round in shape.

Pencil Pod Wax — This well known variety is still the most popular because it seems to stand more adverse conditions than any other variety of bean. It is a vigorous grower, taking only 45 days from seeding until picking. Pencil Pod Wax is not early as susceptible to disease as similar varieties. This is the variety for early Spring planting, since it is less affected by weather conditions. Pods are 6 inches in length, slightly curved near the top, round clear yellow, absolutely stringless and of high quality.

Lima beans

For the average home gardener, the bush lima beans are much easier to grow than pole limas as the plants do not need support. Lima beans are a very popular vege-

table when bought fresh frozen in the grocery store, but for some reason or other they are not too widely grown in the home garden. This is unfortunate because they are a wholesome vegetable which will add considerable variety to the Summer and Fall diet. They require the same soil conditions as snap beans and the earth should contain a good supply of both humus and fertilizer.

The seed will not germinate correctly if the ground is cold and wet so delay planting until the ground is sufficiently warm, which can be anywhere from the first to the middle of June. In any case, do not plant before June 1st. The seeds require a minimum of 65° soil temperature and five days in which to germinate.

Sow the seeds in hills, allowing 2 to 3 beans to each one, making the hills 5 to 6 inches apart. The seeds should be 2 inches deep and the rows 30 inches apart.

Like all other vegetables, it is advisable to dust or spray the vines once a week or ten days with an all-round insecticide and fungicide.

The best harvesting time is when the seeds have reached their full size in the pods, but are still young and tender. At this point, they will be excellent for eating, freezing or canning.

Fordhook No. 242— one of the most popular varieties of bush lima beans with the home gardener. The plants will produce well under adverse circumstances due to a built-in resistance to high temperatures. This variety is a heavy yielder of pods 3 to 4 inches long, each of which contains 3 or 4 thick beans. Fordhook No. 242's flavor is very palatable whether fresh, canned or frozen. 75 days after the seed is sown, the beans are ready for harvesting.

Burpee's Fordhook—Another leading variety of bush lima beans whose dry, mealy quality and flavor is not unlike the sweet chestnut. Pods are 4 to 4½ inches long, 1 to 1⅛ inches wide and ¾ of an inch thick. They are dark green in color and packed with 3 to 4 large plump beans. Plants are bushy, upright, vigorous and spread 2 feet across. This variety also takes 75 days from the time the seed is sown until the beans are ready for picking.

Henderson Bush Lima—An old stand-by variety of baby lima beans which will give you beans 10 days earlier than either Fordhook No. 242 or Burpee's Fordhook. The Henderson bush lima is fine for fresh use, canning, quick freezing and makes a fine, dry shell bean. The pods contain 3 to 4 flattish green, small beans, which turn creamy white when dry. The flavor is fine, making it a very popular variety.

Henderson Bush Lima beans

80

Beets

Here we have what might be called a dual-purpose vegetable. When the plants are young the leaves can be used as especially delicious and tender greens. The round roots can be eaten from the time they are half grown until reaching full size. The younger they are the more tender and tastier the roots.

Beets are classed as a half hardy vegetable which simply means that the seed can be sown in the early spring just as

The Ruby Queen beet can be harvested 43 days after planting

soon as the soil is workable. Late summer sown beets can be left in the ground in the Fall until the time of the hard frosts. At that time they are removed from the soil, their tops cut off and the roots stored in the same type of storage you would use for potatoes.

The type of soil in which they are grown is not too important for beets. It is true they seem to grow best in a light sandy loam, but they will also give good results in almost any type of soil providing it contains plenty of humus and plant food.

The most common mistake made in growing beets is to sow the seed too thickly. It is an easy one to make because the beet seed is really dried and shrivelled fruits in which are embedded as many as 7 or 8

seeds. With this in mind set the so-called "seeds" 2 inches apart. For early Spring sowing, place the seeds 1 inch deep, increasing this to 2 inches deep when planting during the hot weather.

Thin when the plants are about 3 or 4 inches high, for this first thinning, leave the plants 1½ to 2 inches apart then alternate plants can be removed for greens before they crowd each other in the row.

Home gardeners who want an extra early crop of beets can start them indoors in March and then transplant to seedling flats 2 inches apart when the seedlings are 2 inches high. These can be set outdoors at the same time you make your first sowing in the garden. In transplanting the beets to the garden, be sure to make the holes deep enough so that the tap roots of the beets will go straight down, rather than being doubled up underneath.

A month after sowing, feed with a complete fertilizer at the rate of 2 pounds per 50 square feet of row. Depending on the condition of your soil, you may need to make a further feeding 3 or 4 weeks later.

Ruby Queen —This takes 43 days from the time the seed is sown until Ruby Queen reaches the harvesting stage. This early round, dark red-skinned beet is popular for its fresh appetizing appearance which is provided by its deep crimson, sweet and tender flesh. Tops are a short 10 inches in length and colored dark green turning to red.

Beets are a dual purpose vegetable

Burpee's Red Ball has outstanding sweet flavor

Burpee's Red Ball—Outstanding for its tasty, sweet flavoured dark red flesh which is free from woody fibre. Even after cooking its intense, deep red color is well retained. Roots are of uniform globular shape, averaging about 3 inches in diameter at maturity. The tops grow to a medium height and are colored both red and green. Takes 60 days to mature from the time the seed is sown.

Detroit Dark Red Short Top is the most widely grown beet for main crop and Fall use whether for the table, canning or freezing. Tops average 3 inches shorter than those of the regular Detroit Red Strain, which allows you to grow more beets in the row. The roots are also slightly smaller and more globular. The skin is dark red, the flesh sweet in flavor and colored a uniform deep red. 60 days to maturity.

Early Wonder — This is the kind to grow when starting off beets indoors for extra early cropping in the garden. Tops are small and erect, roots are blood red and semi-globular with small tap roots.

Asparagus

Asparagus is a vegetable which can be grown easily in any garden, large or small. The results you get from this edible and long living perennial will be in direct proportion to how carefully and how well you prepared the planting bed.

The part of the asparagus plant we eat is all vegetative growth and this means that the soil must contain lots of "push" in order to stimulate and create this growth.

An asparagus bed correctly prepared will last from 10 to 15 years at least.

Dig that humus — Asparagus is a deep rooted plant requiring a fertile soil containing lots of humus. Sandy loams are the best, but a very light sandy soil is also satisfactory although it will require extra amounts of humus and fertilizer to ensure regular heavy crops. There is not much point in planting asparagus in a heavy clay soil that is poorly drained.

The soil in which you plant asparagus should be free from weeds, especially twitch grass (sometimes called couch grass) and other perennial weeds.

Bearing in mind the long life of this excellent vegetable and the complete occupation of the soil by the plant, the soil must be very carefully prepared. The preparations are best carried out the year before planting, but this is not absolutely essential. In preparing the soil, dig or work into it plenty of humus. Ten bushels of humus per hundred square feet of bed area will not be too much. At the same time, add to the soil a complete fertilizer at 4 pounds per hundred square feet. Mix the humus and the fertilizer thoroughly with the top 8 to 10 inches of soil.

Planting — Well-grown one year plants are considered best for planting. Be sure to discard those with very small crowns along with all damaged and withered plants. Keep the roots covered with a moistened piece of burlap or in a bucket partially filled with water to prevent drying out while awaiting planting.

Early Spring planting is best. You first of all dig a furrow 8 to 10 inches deep and wide enough to accommodate the root system. In the bottom of each furrow scatter a small quantity of complete fertilizer. Cover this with an inch or two of soil mix-bottom of the furrow. They should not be covered originally by more than 2 inches of well firmed soil. As the new plants grow taller the furrow is gradually filled. The rows should be spaced 4 feet apart.

Cultivate regularly during the first season after planting and succeeding ones, to keep the weeds under strict control. Spray or dust the plants every ten days with an all-purpose insecticide or fungicide to keep insects like the "asparagus beetle" and disease under control. Leave the tops standing over Winter.

The next Spring, and each succeeding

An asparagus bed, correctly prepared will last from 10 to 15 years

shallow pan of water they will keep their fresh flavor for several days.

Waltham Washington— Its spears are large and tender, and the tips remain tight until quite tall. Color is dark green with a purplish tinge. Waltham Washington will produce up to 30 percent more stalks than the standard kinds. The flavor is superb.

Paradise Asparagus — A newer rust-proof variety. It is a high yielder and develops extra big and delicious tips for many weeks. The flavor is excellent.

Mary Washington is the tried and proven variety which always produces an excellent crop of spears. You will find it a strong grower with the spears being a lovely green in color, rich in flavor and very tender.

Cucumbers

one, apply a complete fertilizer at the rate of 4 pounds per 100 square feet and work it lightly into the soil on both sides of the rows. At the same time, apply humus to the soil to keep up the supply of organic matter. Apply it at the rate of 6 bushels ture before setting the plants. This prevents the roots from being burnt by direct contact with the fertilizer. By this method much-needed phosphate and potash are added to the lower soil layers. Such deep placement of fertilizers is not practical after the crop is established nor is deep plowing or cultivation.

In heavy clay soils the crowns should be not more than 6 inches below the surface of the soil; in light sandy soil 8 inches will be the correct depth.

The young plants are spaced 18 inches apart, with their roots spread out in the

per hundred square feet of asparagus bed area.

Most people are unable to stop themselves from cutting the spears (the edible tops of the plants) the second year, although this is harmful. For home gardeners without too much will-power a cutting period of a week to 10 days does not seem to do too much harm. Cut the spears when they reach 6 or 7 inches in length with a sharp knife. Usually the cut is made 1 to 1½ inches below the surface of the soil. Be careful in doing this so you avoid injuring nearby developing young spears.

Cut asparagus spears lose their quality very quickly if exposed to warm drying conditions. Best plan is to cut them and cook them immediately. However if kept in a refrigerator or some other cool place and if the bunches are set on end in a

For the really small gardens, cucumber vines require too much space for the value they give. However, there is a way of handling them, and that is to let them climb along a fence, or trellis. In the medium size and larger gardens cucumbers are a most useful vegetable to grow.

Cucumbers require a very fertile soil containing lots of humus and plant food, and need a position which gives them full sunshine. There is no advantage in planting cucumbers out too early, because they are not only especially sensitive to even the slightest frost, but require warm weather for good development.

Cucumbers are sown in so-called "hills" after the danger of frost is past. The hills should be five feet apart and planted with

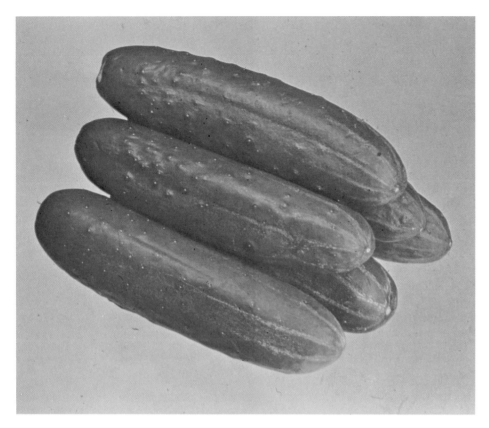

Frequent harvesting helps lengthen the fruiting season of the vines

troubled with that after taste which some persons experience.

Frequent harvesting, which means removing each fruit before the seeds begin to harden and the color begins to change to yellow, will definitely help to lengthen the fruiting season of the vines.

Burpee Hybrid — There seems little doubt that Burpee Hybrid is the finest slicing cucumber for all purposes. High resistance to mosiac and downy mildew are the outstanding attributes of this true F1 hybrid, white spine, slicing type cucumber. The yielding ability of this hybrid has been increased many times over the standard varieties. Vines are extremely vigorous, long lived, and bear an abundance of well-formed, straight, dark green fruits of handsome appearance. They will grow 8 inches and more in length, and $2\frac{1}{2}$ inches wide. The cucumbers are square at both ends with a medium seed cavity and a crispy white flesh of excellent quality.

Burpee Hybrid is one variety that should be planted early, as soon as possible after

six seeds in each, $1\frac{1}{2}$ inches deep. After the plants come through the ground, thin to 3 plants per hill.

A two or three-week jump on the season can be achieved by sowing the seeds that much earlier, and protecting them from cool soil and the possibility of light frosts at night, by covering them with hotcaps or some other type of polyethylene or plastic cover.

Cucumber vines, the small plants in particular, are very susceptible to various insects and disease, so will need dusting or spraying with an all-purpose insecticide and fungicide every week or 10 days from the time the first leaves appear.

Cucumbers can be harvested at almost any stage, depending on the purpose for which the fruits are intended. Different sizes can be picked at the same time, small ones for sweet pickles, the larger for bread and butter pickles, slicing or dills. Many home gardeners prefer to plant the larger fruited varieties for table use, and the pickling types for gherkins, relishes or pickles.

When cucumbers are sliced unpeeled, they usually make for a more attractive salad, and it has been said that if you eat them with the skin on you may not be

Cucumbers can be harvested at different times

Radishes

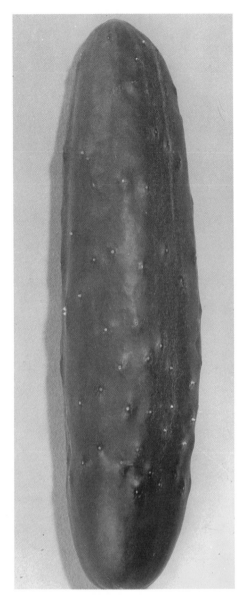

Cucumbers require a fertile soil

Radishes are primarily cool season vegetables and so will not thrive too well during summer heat. They grow best in loose, friable soil, rich in humus and plant food. The small varieties of radishes are ready for use more quickly after they are sown than any other vegetable. It normally takes 3 to 4 weeks under good conditions of soil and weather. The average home gardener usually makes the mistake of planting too many radishes at the one time. They remain edible such a short time that successive sowing of 3 or 4 yards of row should be made every 10 days or two weeks until the middle of June.

Plantings can be resumed again about the middle of August to provide Fall crops

Radishes are cool season vegetables

Scarlet Globe is an early variety

Cherry Bell — Produces early, taking only 22 days from the time the seed is sown until the radishes are ready for eating. It produces round, smooth red radishes $\frac{3}{4}$ of an inch across which resemble cherries in shape and color. Flesh is white, crisp and firm. Cherry Bell retains its good eating qualities for a long time. The radishes have attractive color, ideal shape, extra early maturity, slender tap roots and short tops.

Champion — This type takes 28 days from seeding to harvesting. Radishes have a clear, bright scarlet skin and are round or ball-shaped. The white flesh remains

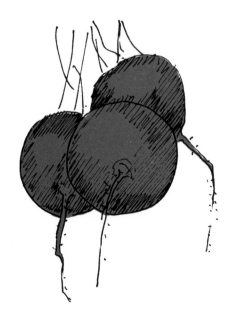

the soil is thoroughly warm. This variety, like other cucumbers is a natural climber, and may be grown on a fence or trellis to supply your needs from a small area. You will be picking cucumbers of the Burpee Hybrid 60 days after the seed is first sown.

Mandarin — The earliest of all cucumbers, taking only 45 days to produce fruits after planting. Because of its earliness, it is one of the best cucumbers for the home garden. As the name suggests, it originally came from China, and because of this has proved to be resistant to blight. By letting the vines climb a trellis or fence it will bear for a particularly long season. Two plantings 20 days apart will furnish the table with salad cucumbers all Summer long.

of crisp, tender radishes.

It is true that radishes can be sown in the hot summer months and grow successfully, but their taste is usually so pungent or hot, they are not palatable.

Sow the seed $\frac{1}{4}$ to $\frac{1}{2}$ inch deep in rows about 1 foot apart. Sowing can commence just as soon as the soil is easily workable in the Spring.

Thin the early, round varieties to stand 1 to 2 inches apart.

There are white radishes of good eating quality

crisp and delicious without becoming pithy, even when the roots reach the diameter of a quarter or larger. As with all large radishes, sow the seed thinly in the beginning, and then thin the plants to stand 2 inches apart in the rows.

Scarlet Globe — Another early variety of radish with excellent quality. They are perfectly globe shaped, with a thin tap root and a uniform bright scarlet color. The even tops are just the right size for bunching. This variety is very uniform at maturity and if not planted too close together, can be harvested in one pulling. Home gardeners who are lucky enough to have a cold frame will find this an excellent strain for forcing. Flesh is crisp, tender and of fine quality.

Lettuce

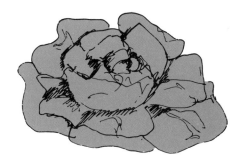

Loose leaf or loose head

Loose leaf or loose head is usually the best type of lettuce for home garden use, especially where the Summers are hot. This type has a long season and a very high nutritional value. The plants form a large,

round thick bunch of leaves which are blanched to a light green or creamy yellow in the center of the plant. Leaves are attractive in appearance, tender and of delightful crispness and mild flavor. You can start to use the thinnings for salads when the plants are just a few inches tall.

Both the loose leaf and the heading varieties of lettuce have a root system which leaves much to be desired. This means the soil should contain plenty of humus and fertilizer so that the roots will have a good supply of plant food close by. The humus will ensure that there is also enough moisture available to the plants.

The best way to grow the loose leaf varieties is to sow the seed in the open just as soon as the soil is workable and then follow this up with a succession of plantings every two weeks until the 1st of July.

Sow the seed in drills or furrows about $\frac{1}{4}$ inch deep and making the furrows about 12 inches apart. Once the seed has germinated, and the lettuce plants are 3 to 4 inches high start thinning, using the thinnings for salads.

Finally, the lettuce plants should be thinned to one foot apart. Most home gardeners go wrong in not doing enough thinning.

Black Seeded Simpson — Probably the most widely grown of all varieties for the home garden, taking just 45 days from the time the seed is sown until ready for picking. It is a hardy variety, and has extra fine quality. This splendid non-heading or cutting lettuce has broad light green frilled and crumpled outer leaves. The center leaves blanch almost white. Its texture is brittle and crisp, the flavor delicate and appetizing.

Salad Bowl — is gaining in popularity every year because of its resistance to heat and its decidedly crisp and tender leaves. The leaves are large, medium green, slow bolting, non-heading and deeply lobed. The mature plants have a definitely resemblance to endive. Salad Bowl will be ready for eating 45 days after the seed is sown.

Ruby — Worth growing in the garden for its unusual color, as well as its sweet and succulent leaves. The bright green, frilled leaves are prominently shaded with intense red which makes this crisp lettuce

85

A fresh head of Burpeeana lettuce

Head Lettuce

In all but the cooler parts of the country the home gardener will be unable to grow head lettuce from seed, because there will not be time for heads to form before the hot weather arrives. Best way for the home gardener to sow this type is to buy plants in veneer plant bands or peat pots ready for setting out in the garden the first of May. It will take about a month from then until the heads are full size and ready for eating. Head lettuce requires a very rich soil containing lots of humus and plant food and will not tolerate dry weather.

Penn Lake — It produces attractive heads of excellent quality and stands up fairly well in hot weather. The outer leaves are dark green and resistant to tipburn. The inside leaves are crisp and firm.

Great Lakes No. 659—A late, vigorous strain which is now used extensively for the second planting of lettuce. Heads are large, round, very firm and completely covered by over-folding, extra fringed, dark green leaves. It is particularly resistant to cold damage, and has seldom been known to sunburn or tipburn. Can be seeded in June and July for a late crop, since by the time the plants are starting to develop heads, the hot weather will be gone and will cause no trouble in this regard.

Cornell 456 (or Imperial 456) — This strain was originally developed for the large commercial lettuce-growing areas on muckland, but it is now found to give excellent results on high ground. The heads are large, solid, heavy and uniform. Leaves are a delightful light green in color. This strain will produce well under adverse conditions.

a delight to the eye and will add much color to summer salads.

Boston or Butter head lettuce—This type of lettuce develops well-folded heads of good form, and resembles a small cabbage in appearance. The hearts are tightly folded and blanch to a light golden, or buttery yellow. In the hot weather parts of the country these varieties may not head as readily as the true head lettuce varieties, but will grow rapidly and produce tender, tasty leaves.

White Boston — 80 days after the seed is sown you will be able to eat this variety. The solid heart blanches to an attractive bright, creamy yellow of high quality and texture. The large heads are tightly folded over the top. Outer leaves are a uniform light green color and are entirely free from brown markings or reddish tinge.

Burpeeana Lettuce — The heads of this variety are small, and ideal for serving as individual salads. The outer loosely folded leaves are dark green, the inner ones blanching to a golden yellow. It is always crisp and without any bitterness. Even the outer leaves retain their crispness and delicate appetizing flavor.

Salad Bowl is resistant to extreme heat

Onions

In the home garden, onions are best grown either from sets or from started plants which are available at garden and nursery centers. Both of these can be set out in the garden just as soon as the soil is workable.

The onion sets provide the familiar green onions for salads or eating by themselves, and the started plants give us the large onions for cooking or slicing.

Plant the sets 2 inches apart in rows 12 inches apart, leaving the tip of the set just above the ground.

With the extra-large Spanish onions, the plants should be set 4 to 5 inches apart to provide plenty of room for them to grow.

Ebenezer — An exceptionally mild-flavored onion which is used extensively for the production of Dutch sets.

Sweet Spanish — This is the best large-sized onion for the home gardener to grow. The onions are large in size and very mild in flavor. They are globular in shape, and a deep amber in color. Flesh is white and firm. If planted in good soil conditions, the bulbs will often attain a very large size weighing over one pound, and from 4 to 6 inches in diameter. The sweet Spanish onion will last in storage until the following Spring.

Carrots

Carrots first came to North America via the colonists who landed at Jamestown, Virginia in 1609, but strangely enough they did not become a basic part of our diet until almost 300 years later.

Although they are high in nutrition, low in cost and always available, it was not until the 1920's that the versatile and colorful carrot became part of everybody's diet. Today they are grown in nearly every country in the world, and North Americans eat them at a rate of 2 million pounds every year. Carrots have an added advantage in being just about the least perishable of vegetables and are a major source of Vitamin A, which is essential to good vision.

Carrots, like beets, parsnips, radishes and turnips produce the part we eat in the soil, and this means that the earth must be loose and friable. Carrots do best in light sandy loams where they usually require very little thinning. However, by choosing the correct variety and by digging plenty of humus into the soil we can use almost any kind, heavy or light. If the soil in your garden is on the heavy side, you should dig into it humus at the rate of 10 bushels per 100 square feet of garden area. Any of the types of humus mentioned earlier in the book will be excellent for this purpose.

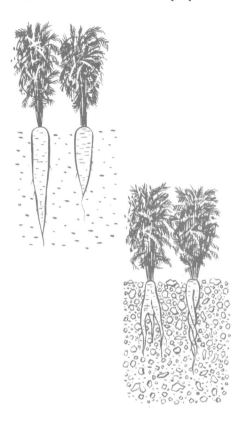

Carrots do best in light sandy soils, in heavy soils they will often be distorted

There is another reason for making the soil as loose and friable as possible, and that is because the seedling carrots are delicate and slow growing. Any soil that contains large pieces of earth, stones and trash will usually result in misshapen roots and unsatisfactory yields. In heavy soils, it is better to grow the shorter varieties of carrots such as Nantez or Chantenay. These two varieties produce carrots that are only 6 or 7 inches long and do not twist or deform their roots in heavy soils.

The storage of sugars and starches in root crops like carrots calls for a plentiful supply of potash in the soil. This is the plant food element which is needed in larger than average quantities by carrots. At the same time as the humus is worked into the soil, a complete fertilizer high in

The Sweet Spanish Onion is the best large onion for home gardeners to grow

87

Carrots are not damaged by early frost

the rows after thinning.

Most varieties of carrots take from 70 to 75 days to reach maturity, but the tastiness of a Fall crop of tender home grown carrots is hard to resist, and no doubt you will start using them long before they reach maturity. However, the carrots can be left in the ground until immediately before freeze up time to give the home owner sufficient carrots for winter storage. For most areas the last safe date for planting would be some time during the month of July. Best way of figuring this out is to take the number of days that a variety uses up from the time the seed is sown until maturity and subtract that from the average date of the first hard frost. Fortunately, carrots are not hurt by the early light frost and so they have a fairly long Fall season.

Scarlet Nantes (Coreless) — The best all round variety for the home gardener to plant, as it will grow equally well in heavy clay or light sandy loams. Roots

potash should be added to it before the seed is sown. Apply this at the rate of 4 pounds per 100 square feet.

Carrots require a location which gives them practically full sun so they will be able to develop and grow in the correct way. Since they are relatively shallow rooted, they will need a lot of water, especially when the weather turns dry and hot. It is a mistake to let the upper six inches of soil dry out as the carrots will not be nearly as large as they should and the quality much poorer.

Immediately before planting, rake the part of the garden where you intend to sow carrot seed several times until the soil is in a finely pulverized condition, removing all bones, stones, sticks and other debris. Sow the seed $\frac{1}{4}$ of an inch deep in rows not less than 12 inches apart, then firm the soil over the newly planted seeds. You will discover that germination is slow and takes about 14 days. It is most important that the seed is sown thinly, because carrots that are too crowded will grow slowly and be poorly shaped. To disturb the roots as little as possible, any thinning required should be carried out when the plants are only 2 to 3 inches high. Thin the carrots to 2 inches apart making sure to firm the soil around the plants left in

Burpee's Golden Heart has a delicate, sweet flavor

Chantenay is a widely used variety

recommended that this carrot be grown in heavy soils. It needs a light sandy loam because of its extra length. The carrots are rich orange in color, smooth skinned, slender and streamlined. They grow 8 to 9 inches long and are $1\frac{1}{2}$ inches in width across the shoulder. The roots are nicely tapered, with a sweet and tender orange flesh.

Chantenay — The most widely used variety for home garden and market, and is the best for winter storage. Chantenay is ready for harvesting 70 days after the seed is sown. It is dependable, highly productive and one of the earliest of the better carrots. The roots are deep orange in color, grow $5\frac{1}{2}$ inches long and $2\frac{1}{4}$ inches thick at the top. They taper towards the bottom to a distinctly blunt or stump end. Flesh is a beautiful rich orange in color, tender, of fine texture and very sweet. Chantenay is splendid for table use, for canning, and keeps excellently in storage.

Burpee's Goldinhart—A special strain of Chantenay which has been selected for uniformity, trueness to type, fine exterior and interior color and a small indistinct core. There is no better variety for freezing. Carrots grow 5 to $5\frac{1}{2}$ inches in length and $2\frac{1}{4}$ inches thick at the shoulder. They taper gradually to a rounded end. Flesh is fine grained, tender and of delicate sweet flavor.

are bright orange in color, cylindrical, blunt ended and measure from 5 to $7\frac{1}{2}$ inches long. Flesh is reddish-orange in color, crisp, tender and has a very delicate flavor. Tops are small and it takes 68 days from planting time until bunching size.

Scarlet Nantes Strong Top — This is probably the best kind to grow in gardens

where the soil is heavy because this variety was bred with a stronger top and this is essential in heavy ground, where the tops break off easily when pulled. The roots are similar in all respects to the above-mentioned regular strain of Scarlet Nantes.

Gold Pak — Valuable for the table, freezing and canning purposes. It is not

Carrots are a source of Vitamin A

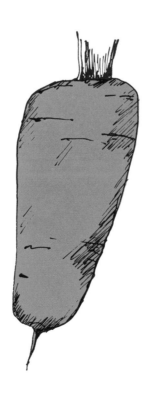

Carrots need a lot of water

89

Corn

There are many varieties of corn available

It is doubtful if there is any vegetable which is more popular at the dinner table than sweet corn. There is a constant demand from most members of the family for this delectable vegetable from the start of the season until it is over.

A check through a seed catalog will show there are a great many varieties on the market, so many that the home gardener, and especially the beginner, can be really confused. In this book we have made a selection of those varieties which are considered to have special merit. They will best fill your requirements for a steady supply of taste delighting sweet corn throughout the season.

Some older home gardeners say that the hybrid varieties which have now completely replaced the former open pollinated kinds do not have the flavor of such old time varieties as Golden Bantam and some of the other kinds they used to grow. This is misleading, for the new hybrids are superior in both yield and quality.

Sweet corn will only grow well in warm, well-drained soils containing plenty of humus and plant food. As a matter of fact, the soil can hardly be too rich for corn.

Before planting we recommend you dig

into the soil humus at the rate of 10 bushels per 100 square feet of garden area. At the same time, work into the earth a complete fertilizer at the rate of 4 lbs. per hundred square feet. There is no doubt that well-rotted barnyard manure is the best type of humus for corn, but this is not always available for most city gardens. The following forms of humus will make satisfactory substitutes: peat moss, materials processed from sewage, discarded mushroom manure or compost.

The ideal time to prepare the soil is immediately before seeding.

Corn seed will rot if put in the soil when cold and wet, so do not try to beat the season. Outdoor temperatures should be in the range of 60 to 70°, and the soil moist.

In most areas, successive plantings at about 10 day intervals from early May to the 12th of July will give a long picking season. The rows are usually planted 3 feet apart and you must have at least 12 rows to ensure correct pollination. Put 4 to 6 kernels in each hill and keep the hills

30 inches apart in the row. For the earliest plantings in the Spring, the seed should be planted only $\frac{1}{4}$ of an inch deep. Later on, this depth can be increased to about 1 inch as the weather turns warm. Corn seed usually requires 4 to 6 days to germinate at a temperature between 65 and 70°.

The sugars in sweet corn rapidly turn to starch in temperatures above 40°, after picking. The best plan is to cook and serve immediately. However if delay is necessary, even for a few hours, keep the corn in the refrigerator.

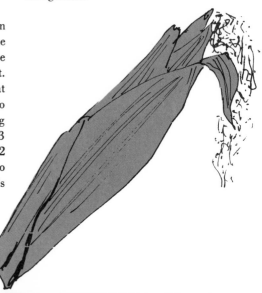

Start cultivating corn when it is 2 to 3 inches high

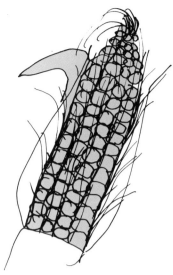

Once the corn plants are 2 to 3 inches high they have to be cultivated frequently to keep the weeds continually under control. Since most of the corn roots are close to the surface of the soil, cultivation should be shallow so as not to injure the roots. As the plants grow it is advisable to hill them up so they will be anchored securely in the soil and will not be as liable to blow over during windy days.

Sweet corn has to be harvested in what is called the "milk" stage. This occurs when the kernels exude a thick milk upon being crushed with the thumb nail. The best stage will have passed when the contents of the kernel appear dough-like or starchy.

Spancross — Undoubtedly Spancross is

The best time to harvest is when a crushed kernel exudes thick milk

Golden Beauty has high yield

the earliest variety to produce, and it will take approximately 58 days from the time the seed is sown until it is ready for eating. Good size, 10 to 12 rowed cobs 7 inches in length are produced. The flavor is very sweet, the quality good and Spancross is resistant to the corn borer.

Golden Beauty — Takes 5 or 6 days longer to produce edible cobs, but the quality is much superior to Spancross. This variety is fast becoming one of the most popular hybrid sweet corn and is very well accepted by home gardeners and commercial growers alike. It is used extensively for the early main season crop. The attractive cobs measure 7 inches in length carrying 12 to 14 rows of kernels usually well filled. These kernels are bright golden yellow in color, and are of excellent quality. Golden Beauty combines high yield and disease resistance.

Carmel Cross — A fine introduction that has become the most popular of the second earliest of the early corns that bear large ears. Eighty days after the seed is

planted, the ears are ready for harvesting. The ears, slightly tapered at the tip, average 7½ inches in length. They contain 10 to 14 rows of delicious yellow kernels of medium breadth and depth.

Seneca Chief — Each year this variety becomes more popular for the main season. It also will produce a crop quite late in the gardening year. The quality is the very finest and the kernels are tender with an excellent flavor. Cobs grow 9 inches long with 12 rows of deep, narrow kernels. Takes 75 days from planting until picking.

Stowell's Hybrid — Many persons, especially late in the season, used to enjoy a white corn called Stowell's Evergreen. In keeping with the current trend of producing and growing nothing but hybrid varieties, Stowell's Hybrid is gradually replacing Stowell's Evergreen. It is a large-stalked late white corn with even rows of kernels. The stalks are tall, averaging 7 feet in height are vigorous and sturdy. The ears are 8 to 9 inches long and have 16 to 18 rows of kernels.

Cabbage

Red Danish cabbage

All home gardens, except the very smallest, should have a few cabbage plants in them. One of the big problems with cabbages is that the plants you set out generally mature all at the same time, and the quality starts to deteriorate before they can be used. To avoid this choose two or three varieties which do not have the same dates of maturity.

It is true that the home gardener can grow his own plants indoors from seed for early Spring use, or sow the seed outdoors for Fall maturing varieties, but started plants are readily available in practically all sections of the country, both in the early Spring and around the 1st of July for the Fall varieties. These are so inexpensive that it does not pay to grow your own plants.

Earliana — This is usually the first variety on the table, taking just 60 days from seeding to harvesting. Heads are small, deep and round. They grow 4 to 5½ inches across and weigh 2 pounds or more. The cores are short and the heads compact and well-folded. An attractive, medium green color is carried well into the heads.

Golden Acre — The best-known variety of early cabbage which produces good sized heads under adverse growing conditions or in home gardens where the soil is not as rich as it might be. Heads are

A well developed cabbage should be 4 to 5½ inches across

well-rounded, compact, 6 inches in diameter and weigh 3½ to 4 pounds each. It is hard to surpass the quality of Golden Acre. Takes 65 days from the time the seed is sown until the heads are ready for table use.

Penn State Ball Head — This is a special strain of the old reliable variety, Danish Ball Head. This is the variety to grow for Fall use or winter storage. Heads are almost globular, 6 to 7 inches deep and 7 to 8 inches across. They are extremely hard and weigh 6 to 7 pounds each. This variety is particularly fine as an excellent Winter keeper, and also makes a tasty sauerkraut.

Golden Acre cabbage

92

A field of Danish Ballhead cabbages ready for harvesting

A cabbage requires exposure to sun

Varieties which are bush-like in growth take up much less space in the garden than the running kinds, and are especially adaptable to small gardens.

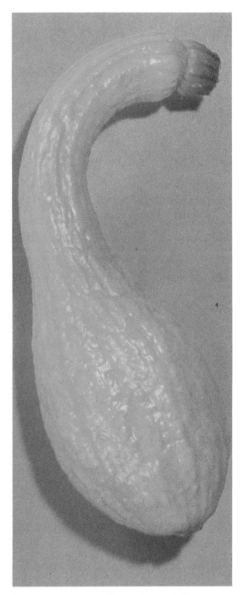

Harvest Summer Squashes while young

Squash

There are two kinds of squash that can be grown in the home garden — Summer squash, which is eaten fresh in the summer; and the kind that is grown for winter storage whose quality is usually better if the outside skin is allowed to form a hard shell. In the descriptions of the recommended varieties the sizes given are those for average fruits when fully grown. However, for best eating, Summer squashes are used while very young and tender. Usually a Summer squash is too old for good eating when the thumbnail does not readily pierce the skin without pressure.

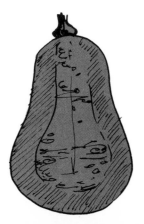

The Italian vegetable marrow

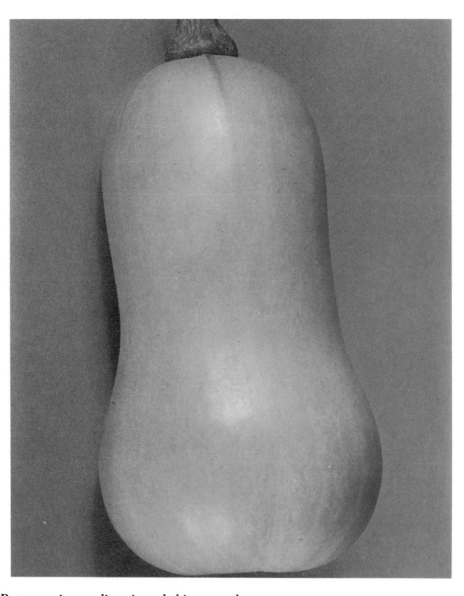

Butternut is a quality winter baking squash

Squash needs the same growing conditions as for cucumbers, in that the soil should contain lots of humus and plant food and they need a position in the garden where they get full sunshine. Do not try to beat the season with squash because they are extremely sensitive to even the slightest touch of frost, and require warm weather and soil conditions in order to start growing well.

Both the Summer and Winter squash are planted in hills about 5 feet apart, placing six seeds 1½ inches deep in each hill. After the plants come through the ground, thin to 3 plants per hill. Squash can also be trained to grow along a fence or trellis in gardens where space is limited.

Summer squash
Hybrid Zucchini — Here is a true first generation Fl hybrid which is an early and prolific yielder. Shiny, medium green cylindrical fruits are 12 inches long at maturity, but are at their best eating stage when 6 to 8 inches long. Flavor is excellent and the texture most tender. The bush-like compact plants are medium in size.

Harris Hybrid Cocozelle — This is sometimes called the Italian vegetable marrow, and is particularly delicious when cooked while young. These marrows are best picked and eaten when about 8 inches long. Plants are of the bush type and yield a large crop of long, smooth fruits. These have dark green skins with lighter green stripes. The flesh is a light, whitish-green color.

Early Prolific Straightneck — Fruits are creamy yellow and edible from the

Zucchini is highly popular

time they reach 4 inches in length until they are 14 inches long. This is another bush variety.

Winter squash

Butternut — It is a top-quality baking squash which is ready for eating 100 days after the seed is sown. The pear-shaped fruits measure about 12 inches long by 5 inches. A long thick neck ends in a bulge in which all the seed is contained. This variety is very productive of convenient size fruits which store quite well.

Buttercup — This is a turban-shaped excellent quality Winter squash 4½ inches deep by 6½ inches in diameter. Rind is thin and tough, and it has a small seed cavity. The thick, orange-yellow flesh cooks sweet and dry. Vines are trailing, vigorous and productive.

Table Queen — Is the very popular acorn or pepper squash. It takes 80 days from the time the seeds are sown until the fruit can be picked. Fruits are acorn-shaped, 5 inches long and 4 inches thick. They are deeply ribbed, have a dark green skin and thick orange flesh which cooks dry and sweet. This is an extremely productive variety which will keep all Winter.

Potatoes

Did you ever have the good fortune to enjoy freshly dug new home-grown potatoes? A few hills of early potatoes are certainly worth the effort of growing in the garden, but unless the garden is large, it does not pay to try to grow all the potatoes your family need the year round.

Potatoes will stand the cold weather of early Spring very well, and so it is safe to plant them as soon as the soil is workable. Be like the farmer and buy certified seed which has had to meet rigid high standards. By planting this type of seed potato you will lessen the chances of disease and obtain bigger and better crops.

The potatoes are cut into 4 pieces weighing about 1½ ounces each. Chunky pieces should be planted in preference to those that are wedge-shaped. Each piece must contain several eyes, or no potato plants will develop.

The soil must be prepared deeply before planting. Dig the seed bed at least 10 inches

Delicious sweet and new potatoes

deep for good results. It must also be loose and friable and this is accomplished by working into it a large quantity of humus at a minimum rate of 6 bushels per 100 square feet. At the same time work into the soil a complete fertilizer at 4 pounds per hundred square feet.

Plant the potato pieces 12 to 15 inches apart and 3 to 4 inches deep. When planting more than one row, keep the rows 3½ feet apart.

Choice of varieties will vary considerably in different parts of the country, depending on the climate. Your local seedsman will be able to tell you the right variety to grow for your area. Other good sources of information are your local garden club or horticultural society.

Swiss Chard

Swiss Chard is a wholesome, nutritious and easily grown vegetable. The leaves are cooked and served like spinach, the midribs like asparagus or both, may be cooked together. Many persons use the stalks to make delicious fritters.

In many parts of the country this tasty green is known simply as chard. Actually it is a leafy form of garden beet, but without the enlarged root. This is the ideal vegetable to plant to provide tasty greens all Summer when spinach and other early spring greens have given up on account of the heat.

There are two ways of harvesting chard, you can remove the outer leaves, thus allowing the center and remaining leaves to grow, or the entire plant can be cut off two inches above the ground and new leaves will soon appear. Because of these methods of picking, a single sowing given good growing conditions will continue to yield heavily throughout most of the summer. To ensure a supply of greens until hard frosts, it is best to make two sowings, one in late April and the other in early July. Sow the seeds in rows 16 inches apart, then thin out to 6 inches in the rows.

Fordhook Giant — A tall growing variety having leaves which are a rich dark green. The leaves have a very crumpled appearance, are thick and fleshy making the most tender greens. The pearly white stalks measure 2½ inches across and make a succulent dish when prepared like asparagus.

Swiss Chard can be prepared like asparagus

The broad mid-ribs of the leaves can be used in the same way. The leaves will be ready for use 60 days after sowing the seed.

Lucullus — Some culinary experts give first place to this variety because of its mild spinach-like flavor. Its leaves are large, heavily crumpled and an attractive light green in color. The thick, broad white stalks are splendid for creaming and also make appetizing fritters.

Rhubarb Chard — Anyone with a small garden will welcome this variety of chard, because it has very attractive crimson red stalks which do not look out of place in flower beds, borders and foundation plantings. The coloring of the stalks is a delicate but translucent crimson red. This rich color extends out through the veins into the dark green heavily crumpled leaves. The leaf stalks are particularly delicious and the leaves have a fine sweet flavor.